THE SUPERCHARGED
MERCEDES

HALWART SCHRADER

THE SUPERCHARGED MERCEDES

Translated by D.B. Tubbs

Drawings by Carlo Demand

EDITA · LAUSANNE

Introduction

If Thor, the god of Thunder owned a sports car it would be a 38/250 hp Mercedes. He would really have no choice, for no other model, before or since 1930, has been so stark, brutal and imposing, so altogether Wagnerian, as the SSK except the Works-only SSKL, that sports car extraordinary which won Grand Prix races. The thunder of these cars' exhaust, the blare of their supercharger as the driver put his foot hard down, have become a part of motoring legend. Built on a heroic scale, these cars brought out heroism in their drivers and most of all in Rudolf Caracciola, who won R.A.C. Tourist Trophy on wet roads in 1929, the German and the Irish G.P. in 1930 and the Mille Miglia of 1931 over 1200 miles of open highway. Almost more remarkable was the way he brought his great Mercedes into third place at Monte Carlo, for anything less suitable for the tight twisty round-the-houses course would be hard to imagine. One remembers too the unofficial record of 48 minutes for London to Cambridge established by an undergraduate's 36/220 set about the same time, a record which stood for several years until beaten once and for all by the late Whitney Straight's road-equipped Mille Miglia Maserati which clocked 47 minutes.

My own earliest recollection of a Mercedes dates from about the same time. A girl I knew had an elderly 33/180, the high-built short-chassis predecessor of the 36/220. We were driving peacefully past Chelsea Old church when an Aston Martin came alongside, challenging. The 6 1/4-litre Merc. engine had been ticking over at about 1000 revs — 33 mph. Not deigning to look down, Frankie gently depressed her foot. The burble from the exhaust grew perceptibly quicker. The Aston Martin dropped back. He changed gear. No need for that, said Frankie as we drew away still in top gear. And then for good measure this splendid girl pressed her foot to the floor, the blower came in with a scream and we never saw our adversary again.

The underslung sports models evolved from this 'K' chassis by Dr Ferdinand Porsche were some of the mightiest sports cars of all time both on the circuits and on the road. They also stand very high in the strange new world of automobile investment. An SSK with the large 'Elephant' blower cost its purchaser 352,000 dollars at auction in Los Angeles during 1979. This might well have made it the most expensive motor car in the world; but at the same sale an example of the later, 'softer' pushrod-engined 500 K was to cost (including buyer's premium) 440,000 dollars — such are the vagaries of taste.

In the pages that follow the whole story of the Company's involvement with supercharging is reviewed, from the post-war application of a 'clutch-in' Roots blower to a rejuvenated 1914 Grand Prix engine and similar installations on the firm's rather dull touring models, down to the great days of 1934-39 when supercharged German cars dominated Grand Prix racing. Never has there been a greater, more spectacular increase in engine power than in the days of the '750-kilo' Formula. When Mercedes-Benz returned to G.P. racing in 1934 'monoposto' Alfa Romeo and Maserati cars were giving 210 bhp; by the end of 1937 the Mercedes M 125 engine was putting out 646 bhp, and a G.P. car in record-breaking trim had exceeded 268 mph on the road. The company's love-affair with supercharging lasted exactly twenty years, from 1919 until 1939; and during those two decades Mercedes-Benz built some of the most exciting motor cars of all time. The supercharged Mercedes and the people associated with them, engineers, drivers, pit-staff, film stars — and even politicians — here form the nucleus of a fascinating social history.

D.B. Tubbs

36/220 hp S Mercedes-Benz belonging to the Rowe Sisters, famous dance act of the twenties.

THE SUPERCHARGED MERCEDES 1919-1939

It was Paul Daimler, the son of Gottlieb Daimler the pioneer of motoring, who remarked that 'Mechanical engineering as we know it today is due to the genius of a few men who, confronted with certain discoveries, had the courage and tenacity to transform them into realitys. Paul Daimler himself can be included in that select band, for he was one of the most capable automobile engineers in the early part of this century, and he was instrumental in developing a remarkable idea: a car engine which derived much of its power from a compressor or, more precisely, a system of forced induction.

The idea appealed to enthusiasts from the start. Drivers of fast cars became fascinated by the idea of supercharging, and it was not unusual for them to pay twice the price of an ordinary car for the sake apparently of outside exhaust-pipes and an ear-splitting scream as they accelerated.

However, supercharged engines were not invented simply to provide thrills for the well-to-do: they reflected the study of applied physics by various pioneers who saw, in forced induction, a means of increasing performance. The idea of injecting supplementary mixture into the cylinders over and above what could be drawn in by the suction of the piston had already been put into practice by Gottlieb Daimler in 1895. In a four-cylinder 'horseless carriage' engine patented by him on 3 April of that year the pistons incorporated a valve through which air compressed in the crankcase was to rush in as the piston reached bottom dead centre. The air 'brought in under pressure' as Daimler wrote, would give inproved filling during the induction stroke and thus better combustion, while on the exhaust stroke it would have a scavenging and cooling effect. At that time Daimler was concerned mainly to improve the running of his engine, not to increase specific output.

The origins of the supercharger itself date back to the 1890s. Working at Connersville, near Auburn,

Indiana, in the Middle West of America, far from any industrial centre, the brothers Francis and Philander Roots took out a patent for a blower originally intended to make better use of the water wheel which drove their parents' spinning-mill. During the next forty years this original wooden Roots blower was described and illustrated in magazines throughout the U.S.A., and the blowers were adopted in workshops and factories on the Continent.

In 1902 Louis Renault patented a centrifugal compressor (though he never used one on his cars) and the Swiss designer Marc Birkigt considered using a piston-type blower before 1914, on Hispano-Suiza racing cars. The American Chadwick car must also be mentioned as it was the first to appear in competition with a supercharged engine. This was in 1906 when a Chadwick so fitted entered, and won, the Giant's Despair hill-climb. The Chadwick cars which took part in the William K. Vanderbilt Cup races at Savannah, Georgia, in 1908 were also secretly fitted with superchargers. They were handled by Works drivers. The Chadwick firm lasted only a short time, and disappeared in 1916.

During the First World War the idea of forced induction was revived for use on aero-engines. The density of air decreases with altitude and so, in order to outclimb the enemy it was necessary to counteract this and maintain power at altitude. Initially three-cylinder radial piston-type compressors were used, but the movement of the reciprocating masses being difficult to balance, recourse was had to vane-type compressors like the German Wittig, which, although offering a 50 per cent power increase, proved unreliable in service. In France Rateau centrifugal blowers were adopted, and the Americans too used centrifugal blowers, the Moss, developed by General Electric.

The Wittig vane-type compressor posed grave lubrication problems and the Germans were therefore obliged to explore other systems of supercharging.

Much thought was given to the matter at the Daimler Motoren Gesellschaft in Stuttgart, where aero-engines represented a substantial part of production. By the beginning of 1918 series production of supercharged aeroplane engines began. The compressor chosen took the form of a Roots blower driven from the crankshaft and built in unit with the engine. At the same period, Daimlers were working on super-charged aero-engines for submarines, in which as many as four Roots blowers were mounted in series, thus doubling the output from a six-cylinder aeroplane engine. The Armistice ended these.

By the end of the First World War much useful experience had been gained, in Germany as elsewhere, of the advantages of supercharging. As things turned out, of course, it was neither aero-engines nor submarines which encouraged its future development. Credit for demonstrating the value of forced induction goes to the automobile. The Treaty of Versailles set limits to German activity in various directions, including aeronautics and naval construction, all the more attention, therefore, was given to improving the motor car engine, and here once again the Daimler company played the rôle of pioneer.

During the early twenties 'supercharger' became one of the 'In' words among motoring enthusiasts — although most of them would have had difficulty in explaining exactly what the term meant. Perhaps even today a word or two of explanation may not be out of place, especially as the superchargers we are discussing are no longer used in Formula One racing.

During 1914-1918 supercharged aero-engines were usually referred to as 'high altitude' engines, the Wittig being included in this class. But a supercharger can also do duty as a pump; D.K.W., for instance, used a piston-type compressor on their two-stroke motorcycle and car engines so as to obtain better filling and more complete scavenging of the exhaust gases than mere pre-compression in the crankcase would afford. The device was fitted to the D.K.W. motorcycle and

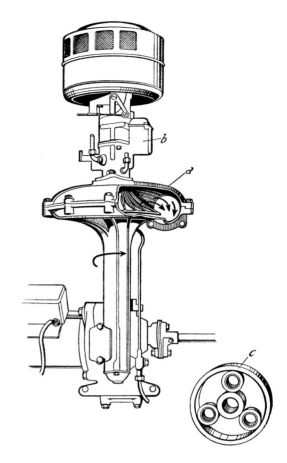

Centrifugal blowers, as fitted by Duesenberg, Auburn, Graham-Paige and others, functioned in the same way as a turbine, the volume of gas delivered being proportional to the rotational speed of the blades (a). The latter, installed between the carburetter (b) and the engine, were driven via planetary rollers (c) which imposed frictional limits on the torque.

This Zoller vane-type blower (a) on a racing Auto Union, is installed between the engine and the carburetter (c). It blows fuel-air mixture into the combustion chambers; the fuel-pump is at (b).

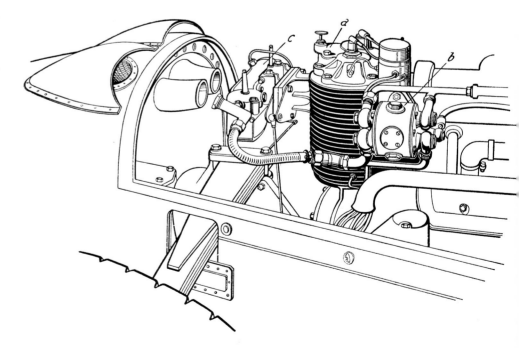

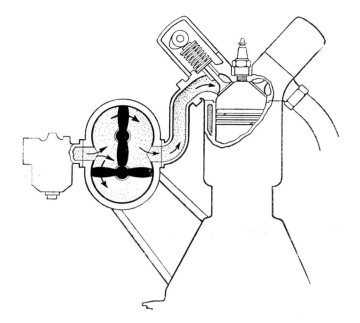

This diagram shows a proprietary supercharger marketed by Derbuel. Rotating paddles suck mixture from the carburetter and force it into the combustion chamber.

The first supercharger fitted by Mercedes was installed experimentally on a 10/30 PS Mercedes-Knight sleeve-valve engine in 1919. Mounted beneath the carburetter and brought into engagement by a clutch, the blower turned at speeds up to 10,000 rpm. Improvised gearing replaced the original dynamo drive.

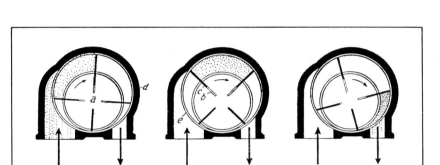

This diagram shows the workings of a sliding-vane compressor of the Zoller or Cozette type. Inside a cylindrical casing (d) is mounted, off-centre, a rotating member (a). This rotor carries radial vanes (c) sliding axially within it. Depending upon the position of the rotor the vanes form a gas chamber of varying volume. The vanes do not touch the housing but rest upon the interior face of a drum (e) which turns with them. Movement of the rotor causes the volume of the chamber to decrease compressing the gas contained in it, forcing it under pressure to or from the carburetter.

Rotary-piston compressors like the Roots blower resemble a gear-type pump. The two figure-of-8 lobes (b) rotate inside a housing (a) with minimum clearances separating them from one another, and from the walls of the housing. The volume of mixture or air compressed is determined by the ratio between the swept volume of the blower and that of the engine.

The engine of the 28/95 PS Mercedes entered for the 1921 Targa Florio, a Six with the cylinders cast in pairs, was fitted with a supercharger of Roots rotary-piston type. The blower now became an integral part of the engine. It was driven by a toothed ring on the flywheel and brought in at will by means of a multiple-disc clutch.

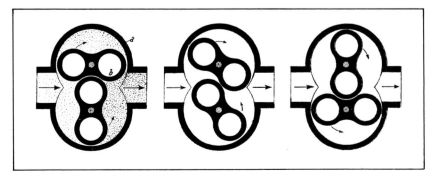

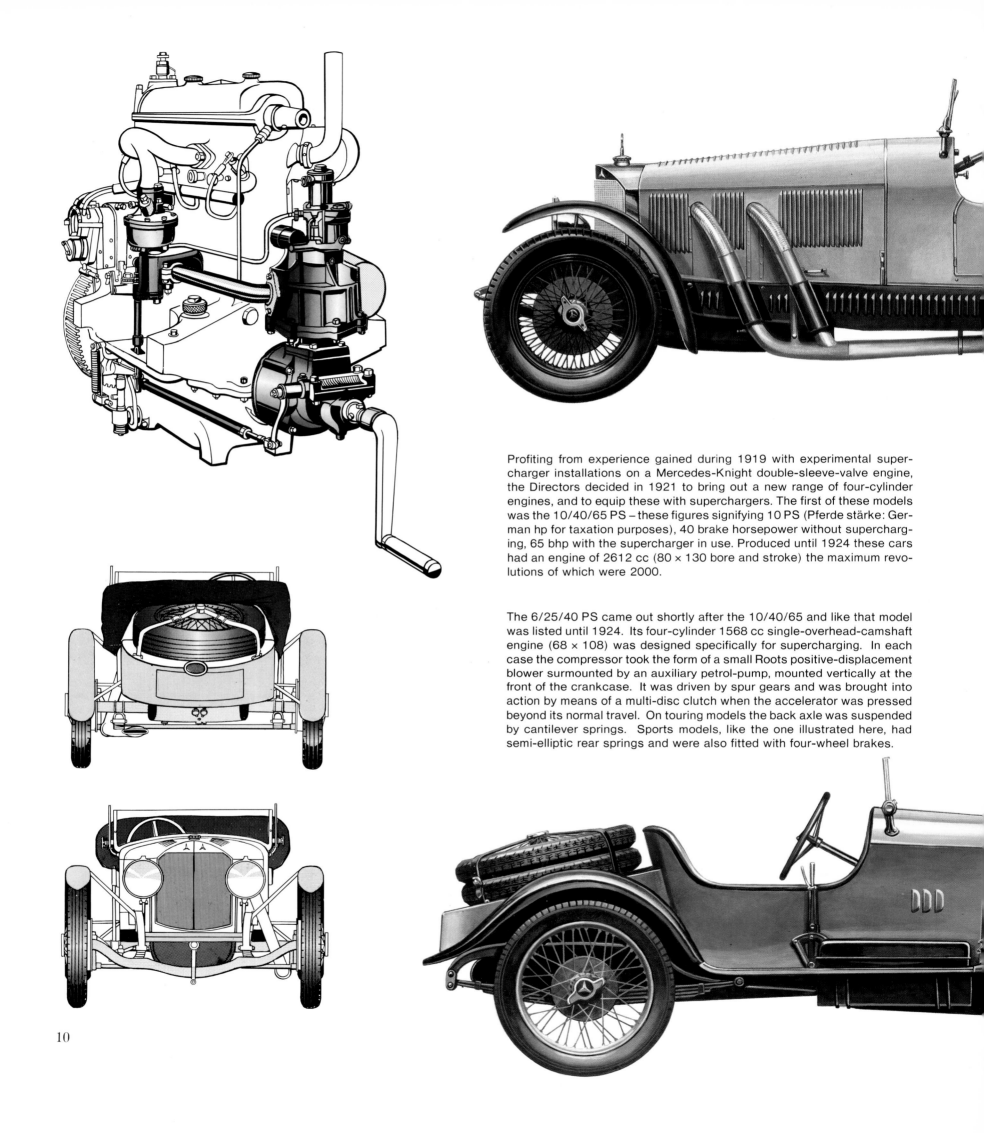

Profiting from experience gained during 1919 with experimental super-charger installations on a Mercedes-Knight double-sleeve-valve engine, the Directors decided in 1921 to bring out a new range of four-cylinder engines, and to equip these with superchargers. The first of these models was the 10/40/65 PS – these figures signifying 10 PS (Pferde stärke: German hp for taxation purposes), 40 brake horsepower without supercharging, 65 bhp with the supercharger in use. Produced until 1924 these cars had an engine of 2612 cc (80 × 130 bore and stroke) the maximum revolutions of which were 2000.

The 6/25/40 PS came out shortly after the 10/40/65 and like that model was listed until 1924. Its four-cylinder 1568 cc single-overhead-camshaft engine (68 × 108) was designed specifically for supercharging. In each case the compressor took the form of a small Roots positive-displacement blower surmounted by an auxiliary petrol-pump, mounted vertically at the front of the crankcase. It was driven by spur gears and was brought into action by means of a multi-disc clutch when the accelerator was pressed beyond its normal travel. On touring models the back axle was suspended by cantilever springs. Sports models, like the one illustrated here, had semi-elliptic rear springs and were also fitted with four-wheel brakes.

Derived from the 6/25/40, two special machines were prepared for the 1922 Targa Florio race, running in the 1¹/₂-litre category, and described as 6/40/65 PS. With a bore and stroke of 65 × 113 (1499 cc) this unit had twin overhead camshafts and four valves per cylinder. The chassis was similar to that of the touring 6/25/40, and used cantilever back springs. One of the two 6/40/65 cars was the subject of aerodynamic experiments in 1922 in course of which two special bodies were built.

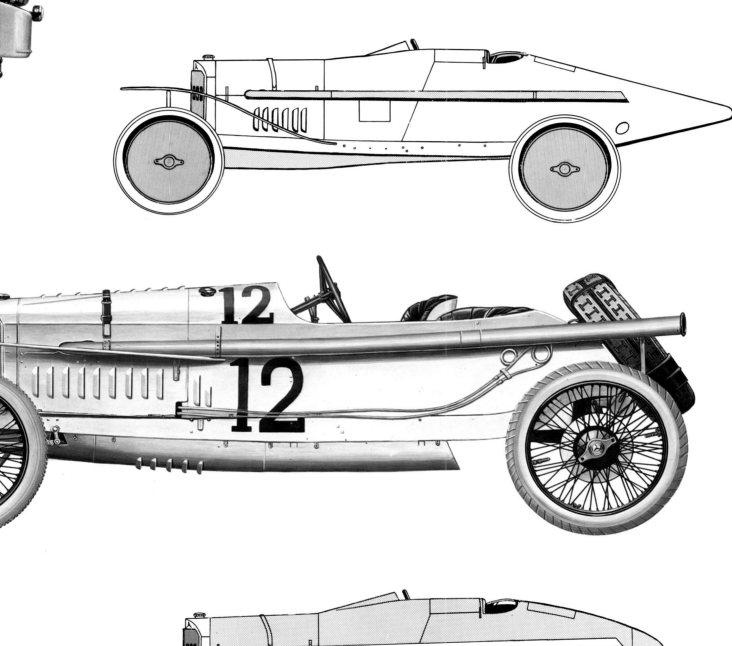

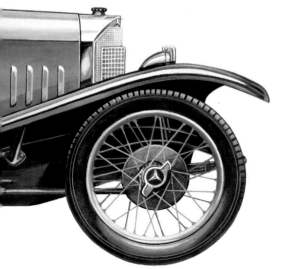

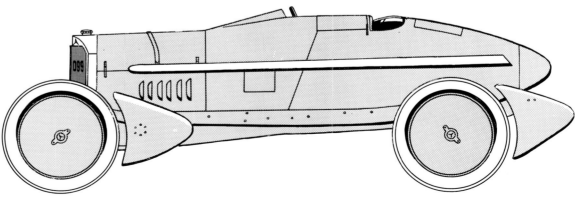

11

also to the four-cylinder car called 4 = 8 and known later as the V 1000, which was built from 1928 to 1932 at Zschoppau.

This was not strictly speaking a compressor but rather a forced induction device which could be inserted into one of the three following categories: 1. blowers having a bladed wheel like a turbine – the centrifugal type of supercharger; 2. compressors utilising inter-meshing paddles, e.g. the Roots blower; and 3. vane-type blowers, which function in much the same way. The drive in each case being taken mechanically from the engine, the blower speed is always proportional to engine revs. The only difference between the three systems lies in the way in which the mixture is led to the combustion chambers. The Roots rotary-piston compressor works on the principle of a gear-type pump, in which the compression of a volume of air or gas is determined by the ratio between the displacement of the compressor and the displacement of the engine. Roots blowers were used by many racing and sports car makers; among them Alfa Romeo, Bugatti, Sunbeam, Delage, Bentley, Fiat and Mercedes-Benz. In the 1930s proprietary superchargers were marketed as accessories by various manufacturers (e.g. Centric in England, Derbuel or V.D. in France) for fitting to ordinary cars.

Centrifugal superchargers work in the same way as a turbine, their output being proportional to the speed of the blades. They are quieter than a Roots blower but less effective at low engine speeds. The centrifugal blower was part of the Duesenberg's renown, and was also fitted to the Miller. It looked like a big metal mushroom sprouting from the side of the cylinder block below the carburetter on big American cars such as Auburn and Graham-Paige. For them to provide sufficient output these ancillaries were always made pretty large; it therefore took quite a lot of power to drive them, say about 20 bhp, of which one-third disappeared in friction losses, leaving the other two-thirds available for compression. The blower

shaft sometimes ran as fast as 23,000 rpm. The supercharger casing was plumbed into the engine's cooling system, allowing the droplets of mixture to vaporise even at low speeds. The output of the Graham-Paige, to take one example, was increased by 35 per cent at least, thanks to a centrifugal blower.

The vane-type supercharger fitted by E.R.A. owed its fame to Dr Arnold Zoller. Externally the type is characterised by a cylindrical housing, inside which is a rotor mounted eccentrically. This rotor carries radial vanes arranged to slide axially within the rotor shaft which, as the rotor turns in its housing form chambers of varying volume. The vanes never actually touch the housing but press against the inside of a drum which rotates with them. As the rotor turns the volume of the chambers enclosed diminishes thus compressing the mixture contained in them. When this volume reaches its minimum the chamber coincides with a delivery port (outlet) in the blower casing. Cozette superchargers popular in France were of this type, and were used on Lea-Francis, Ulster Austin Seven and other British performance cars around 1930, and many French sports models. Other well-known vane-type blowers were the Powerplus with which Captain George Eyston was associated, and the Centric, most popular of British proprietary superchargers which developed into the Marshall.

Theoretically a supercharger may be mounted upstream or downstream in relation to the carburetter – either blowing air into it or sucking mixture from it. From their original 10/30 PS model* of 1919 onwards Mercedes adhered to the former system, except on Grand Prix cars from 1937 onwards, in which the compressor was moved downstream, and sucked instead of blowing.

Paul Daimler in his work on supercharged car engines always declared in favour of the Roots blower. Towards the end of the 1918 war one of these was fitted experimentally to a 4048 cc sleeve-valve 16/50 PS Mercedes-Knight engine developed from the 16/46

---

* The first figure here is the horsepower for taxation purposes, the second purports to be the power actually developed. Fiscal h.p. (called in Germany PS) was calculated at 4 h.p. per litre. A 10 PS car was thus a $2^1/2$-litre.

In a supercharged 28/95 Max Sailer and his mechanic Hans Ricker finished second in the 1921 Targa Florio. They also won the Coppa Florio for best placed production car.

10/40/65 PS Mercedes were marketed from 1921 to 1924. At 19,500 Marks it was a very competitive machine in which owners could more than hold their own at events such as the Baden-Baden meeting won by Mme E. Merck (left) and G. Kluge in 1924.

For the 1922 Targa Florio Max Sailer had a faster 28/95 with lower, longer body. He finished first in the over-4½-litres category and was sixth overall. Mercedes were represented in Sicily that year by seven cars: two 6/25/40 PS entrusted to Minoia and Scheef – first 1½-litre – three 1914 Grand Prix cars handled by Lautenschlager, Salzer and winner, Masetti, plus two blown 28/95 PS for Werner (8th) and Sailer.

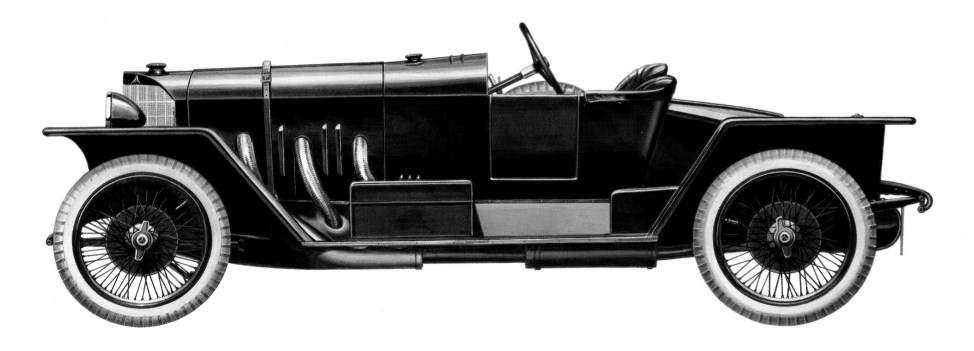

Introduced in 1914 the 28/95 PS Mercedes was originally a large heavy touring car, although its 7520 cc (105 × 140) six-cylinder engine was similar in design to the Mercedes aero-engines being supplied to the German air service. At that stage there was no supercharger and output was given as 95 bhp at 1800 rpm. In 1920 Paul Daimler and Max Sailer undertook the design of a sporting version; they reduced the wheelbase, lowered the radiator and driving positions, and – more important – installed a two-lobed Roots blower, driven by gearing from the nose of the crankshaft. The super-

charged 28/95 thus created developed 140 bhp and had a top speed of nearly 90 mph (shown above is the 1923 model). For the 1921 Targa Florio Sailer built a very stark racing car, the layout of which is shown in the drawing below: semi-elliptic springs with friction shock-absorbers, six-cylinder engine with the cylinders in pairs and an aluminium rocker-box, the blower mounted on the exhaust side. Racing 28/95s were reserved at first for Works drivers; after 1922 a few were supplied to selected private entrants but this was never a catalogued model, unlike the 28/95 Sports.

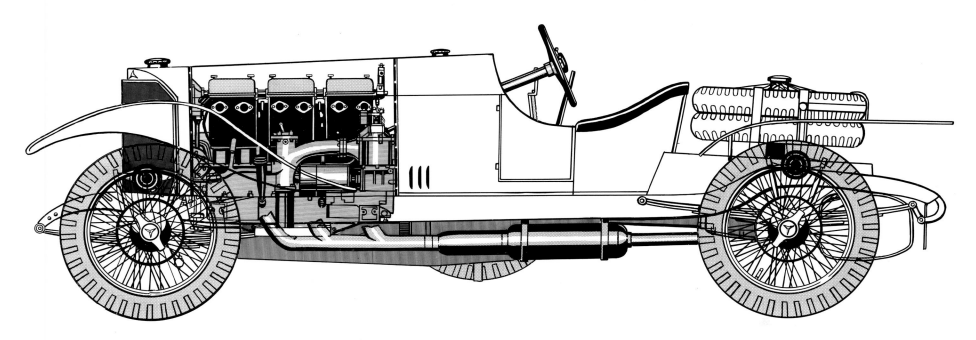

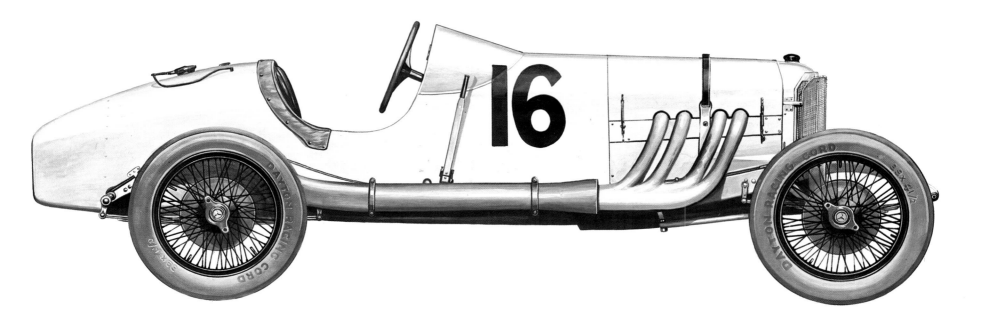

The Indianapolis 500 Miles Race in 1923 was run under the international Grand Prix formula then in force, which allowed a maximum cylinder capacity of 2000 cc. Mercedes spared no pains in their efforts to beat the Americans on their home ground. Both engine and chassis were new. Loosely based on the 10/40/65 PS the four-cylinder 1983 cc power-unit (70 × 129) gave 95 bhp at 4500 rpm; it had twin overhead camshafts and four valves per cylinder. The supercharger was mounted on the nose of the crankshaft, and for the first time in Mercedes history the exhaust manifold was on the right-hand side. Of the three cars on the grid, two crashed, but Sailer and Werner (above) succeeded in finishing – in 8th and 11th places respectively (using the reserve). However the 2-litre proved itself a formidable hill-climb car before winnings its first important race (in 1924), having in the meantime undergone substantial modifications to chassis, engine and bodywork. Werner, driving car no. 10 that year brought off a remarkable double by winning both the Targa Florio and the Coppa Florio. The second supercharged Mercedes, with Alfred Neubauer up, came 15th.

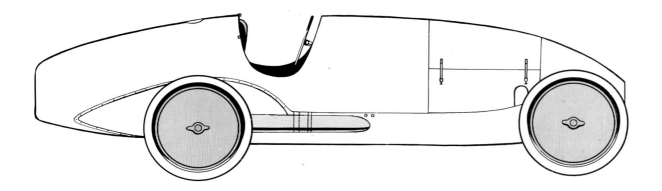

Pursuing their experiments on streamlining begun in 1922 with a 6/40/65, Mercedes engineers in 1923 came up with the special body shown here for one of the 2-litres built for Indianapolis. Although not run in the 500, it was developed into the car with which Otto Salzer won the Koenigsaal-Jilowischt hill-climb near Prague in April 1924.

Ferdinand Porsche made a great many alterations to the four-cylinder engines of the Mercedes entered for the 1924 Targa Florio (opposite), the most obvious of which was a larger and much-finned supercharger. Its power rose from 95 bhp to 126 bhp; by the end of 1924 it was giving 150 bhp at 4800 rpm.

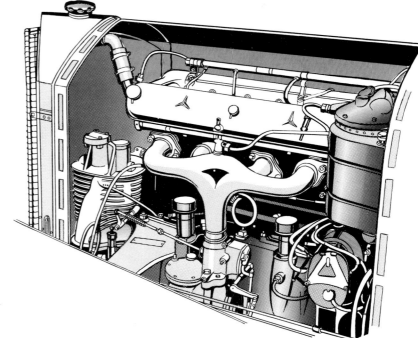

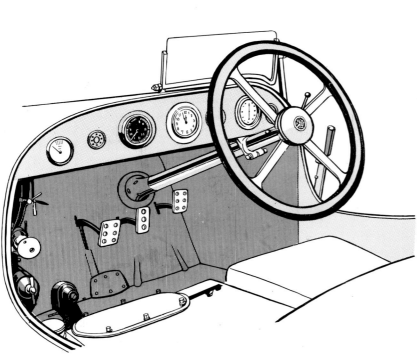

Targa Florio 2-litre 1924. A classic Vintage racing car: outside handbrake, pedals drilled for lightness, drip feeds and aero screen.

The 27 April 1924 was a great day for Mercedes, who once again distinguished themselves at the Taga Florio, Europe's most important and glamorous event in those days. Christian Werner the winner is here seen (right) with Ferdinand Porsche, designer of the car. He covered the 265 miles of precipitous road through the Madonian Mountains of Sicily in 6h. 32m. 27s., at a record speed for the long-established event of 41.02 mph.

The ex-Indianapolis 2-litre supercharged car seen (below) at the pits, was brilliantly prepared by Ing. Ferdinand Porsche, who had joined Daimler-Benz a year previously. Two similar cars finished 10th (Lautenschlager) and 15th (Alfred Neubauer), so that Mercedes romped home with the team-prize and the first three places in the 2-litre class.

Racing the best form of Publicity

PS model of 1909; but this unit proved unable to accept the increased power, lubrication problems demonstrating that the fragile double-sleeve-valve engine was unsuited to supercharging. No supercharged 16/50 PS found its way into the catalogue.

One year later, during the summer of 1919, Daimler instigated work on a supercharged engine for series production. Around mid-September a blower was fitted to another Knight sleeve-valve engine, the 10/30 PS, and at the beginning of October this was installed in a corresponding chassis. Between 17 October and the end of November a team of engineers including Karl Schopper, Jakob Krauss and Walter Schwerdtfeger covered more than 1200 miles in this modified 10/30. The installation comprised a two-lobed Roots blower, a multi-disc clutch and a set of spur gears, the clutch bringing the blower-drive into engagement when the accelerator was fully depressed. However, much remained to be done, and there were delays. The oil in the neighbourhood of the exhaust ports charred instead of lubricating, and the sleeves overheated, leading to breakage of the eccentric-drives. The 10/30 PS was introduced in unsupercharged form. A 2,612 cc four-cylinder giving 35 bhp at 2000 rpm was listed until October 1921, when the Knight sleeve-valve licence was dropped. On the Stuttgart-Echterdingen road meanwhile trials were proceeding of two other supercharged models, this time using overhead camshafts. These cars were introduced shortly afterwards as the 10/45/65 PS and 6/25/40 PS. The latter, as the model-name suggests, was a $1^1/_2$-litre (actually 1,570 cc) giving 25 bhp unblown (at 2800 rpm) but 40 bhp with the blower engaged, i.e., an increase of 60 per cent. The $2^1/_2$-litre 10/40/65 PS with its 25 extra horsepower benefitted even more, to the tune of 62.5 per cent.

When, therefore, the two Mercedes works Grand Prix drivers Lautenschlager and Salzer drove a 6/25/40 PS to the Berlin Motor Show in 1921 they were fully conscious of the privilege, and the model caused quite a stir; but orders came slowly because the high price of the car and the noise from engine kept buyers away. Remembering Lautenschlager's French G.P. victory in 1908 and that even greater day in July 1914 when Mercedes came first, second and third at Lyons, Paul Daimler decided that racing was the best form of publicity. By winning a few major competitions he would soon convince sceptics who claimed that supercharged engines must infallibly blow themselves to bits. The two fixtures chosen were a hill-climb, the Koenigsaal-Jilowischt, and Europe's toughest long-distance race, the Targa Florio.

Wisely, it was decided not to race the new $1^1/_2$-litre. Instead they resurrected the pre-war 29/95 PS, a rugged six-cylinder whose overhead camshaft and general design belonged to the same family as the 6/25/40 PS, since both had much in common with wartime Mercedes aero-engines. Having a bore and stroke of 105 by 140 and 7250 cc it developed 95 bhp from its 7 litres and 28 tax PS at only 1800 rpm. This performance was hardly startling, but the design still looked reasonably modern, and being so lightly stressed would stand supercharging.

The supercharged 28/95 PS came out in 1920, and like the smaller models was fitted with a two-lobed Roots blower built under British licence from Godfrey and Partners. After 1921, Mercedes used their own, design, registered under patent 341485. The blower was driven from the crankshaft, and reached a speed of 9,000 rpm. Unblown a 28/95 would do 76-80 mph; the blower gave it an extra 30 bhp and raised its maximum to almost 90 mph. On 22 May 1921 Otto Salzer took his blown 28/95 to Koenigsaal where, first time out, he made fastest time of the day. His speed for the $3^1/_2$ miles was 55.8 mph, breaking the record.

A week later the Mercedes engineer-driver Max Sailer from Esslingen arrived in Sicily driving an identical car. He too scored a possible. Covering the 330 miles over rough, twisty roads in the Madonian Mountains in 7 h 27 m to average 36 mph, he collected the

Coppa Florio, premier award for production cars irrespective of category. Another fact worth mentioning is that Sailer drove the entire race, plus the journeys from Stuttgart to Sicily and back, on one set of tyres.

For the time being the supercharged 28/95 PS remained a purely competition car handled by works drivers, but the 6/25/40 and 10/40/65 introduced at the 1921 Berlin show went on sale to the public, and remained in the list until 1924. In 1923 the smaller of the two could be supplied with a twin-overhead-camshaft head and at the same time brought within the $1\frac{1}{2}$-litre category for the benefit of private enthusiasts. This was done by reducing the bore from 68 mm to 65 mm and lengthening the stroke from 108 to 113 mm for a capacity of 1,499 cc. On this competition model, as on standard 6/25/40 and 10/40/65 cars the blower could be engaged at will by pressing hard on the throttle. This became Mercedes practice.

The twin-cam version of the 6/25/40 PS had been built with rather more than amateurs in mind. Sailer's Coppa Florio could not be allowed to remain an isolated victory. The Directors determined to do even better in 1922; so they produced yet another cylinder-head, this time with twin overhead camshafts and four valves per cylinder, two inlet and two exhaust. By engaging the blower the engine could be taken to 5,000 rpm for brief periods, producing 75 bhp. The chassis was modified little, except that the cantilever rear springs of the standard model were replaced by semi-elliptics. Two of these cars were taken to Sicily at the beginning of March and entrusted to the well-known Italian driver, Fernando Minoia, and Paul Scheef. The Daimler Motoren Gesellschaft itself was represented by other machines: there were three of the 1914 Grand Prix cars brought up to date and called 115 hp, two painted white for Works drivers Christian Lautenschlager and Otto Salzer, the other Italien red in compliment to its driver, Count Giulio Masetti, winner of the previous year's Targa Florio. This array was supported by Max Sailer and Christian

Werner in supercharged 28/95s, and 2 April that year proved a veritable triumph for Mercedes. Sailer won the over-4.5 litres class and came sixth over all with Werner eighth. Victory went to the Masetti in the red G.P. car and Paul Scheef took first place amongst the *voiturettes* with his 16-valve machine.

An interesting feature of the race was the speed shown by the pre-war but supercharged 28/95 sports models despite their Edwardian design and touring ancestry. Sailer's 28/95 ran faster on the testing Sicilian roads than the other Mercedes, which had, Minoia's excepted, generally more powerful engines. Both Sailer (59.9 kph) and Werner (59.4 kph) proved faster than the white $4\frac{1}{2}$-litre G.P. cars of Lautenschlager (59.2 kph) and Salzer (58.4 kph) entered in the Racing category, while the winner Masetti's red machine averaged 63.1 kmh. These 28/95s, although fairly archaic, did not look quite so innocuous as the mechanically similar machine with which Sailer had won the previous year. The body was lower and longer, an exhaust-pipe hugging the side, and with an engine giving 140 bhp the 1922 cars were faster.

The blown 28/95 had many more victories to come, in the hands of both factory and amateur drivers. In 1922 the Koenigsaal-Jilowischt hill-climb was again won by Sailer who shattered his previous record. The Dutch driver Theodor Wiemann managed to win four separate Classes in the Scheveningen production car race, and a dozen more victories were collected in hill-climbs and races all over the Continent. The model remained current until 1926, sometimes fitted with streamlined bodywork.

Equally successful were the 6/25/40 and 10/40/65. In 1923 the Swedish driver of a 10/40/65, Ake Eklund, won the Swedish Summer Hill-climb Championship and with it the Summer Cup presented by Count Charles von Rosen. One Ernst Saurer in a similar car won the 3-litre class in the international race at Scheveningen and August Momberger was placed first in the Eberstadt-Birkenbach hill-climb and again

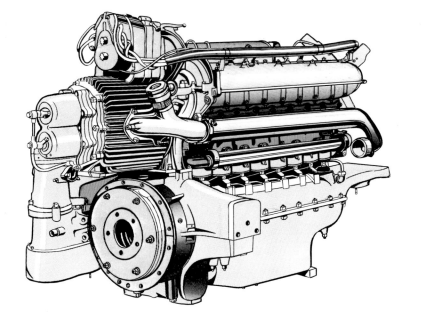

First eight-cylinder designed by Ferdinand Porsche, the M 218 (*M* for *Motor*) was also the first of this type built by Mercedes. Its characteristics were as follows: 1980 cc (61.7 × 82.8), twin overhead camshafts, four valves per cylinder, compression ratio 5: 1, dry-sump lubrication. With its large Roots blower it produced 170 bhp at 7000 rpm, remarkable figures for the period in which it was built.

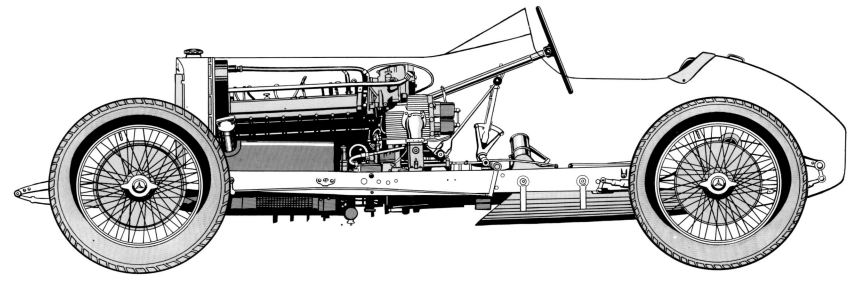

The 128 engine made its debut in the 1924 Italian Grand Prix powering a chassis which, although orthodox enough, had a number of up-to-date features, as this drawing shows. Flanked on its left by an oil-tank holding 24 litres, the engine was mounted well back in the chassis, and formed, with its three-speed gearbox, a rigid ensemble. To obtain the best possible distribution of masses a 'saddle' fuel tank was slung between the frame members and forward of the rear axle, with the propeller shaft passing above it. The blower was liberally finned, and outsized brakedrums were fitted, 20 inches in diameter. In contrast to the two-seater cars which had run the 1924 Italian G.P. those taking part in the German Grand Prix of 1926 were equipped as four-seaters so as to be eligible for the 2-litre Sports category. It was in car no. 14 (below) that young Rudolf Caracciola won his first big victory, which happened also to be the first important race held in Germany since the war.

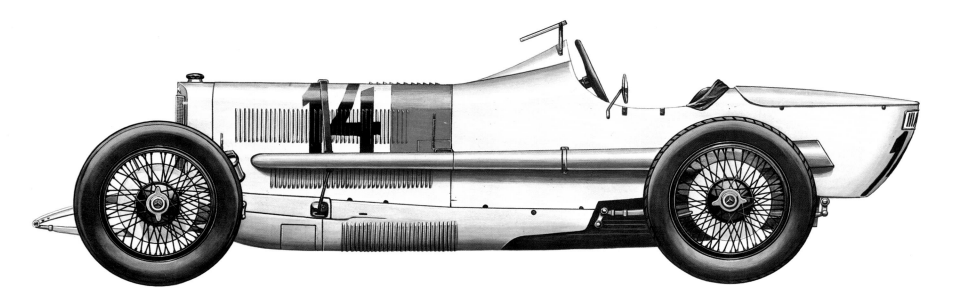

As from 1923 Ferdinand Porsche found himself charged with the construction of a new six-cylinder range of 2 litres, 4 litres and 6 litres capacity, the flagship of which was to replace the 28/95. Announced in 1924 this 24/100/140 – or Type 600 – housed an in-line Six of 6240 cc (94 × 150) with single overhead camshaft developing 140 bhp at 3000 rpm. Six body types were catalogued of which the largest and most stately, a limousine (above) measured more than 5 metres – say 17 feet – over all. Despite a weight of 3300 kg or 66 cwt, the 24/100/140 – sold in Britain as the 33/140

hp – could do between 75 and 80 mph, which enabled sporting versions to figure no fewer than thirty-seven times amongst the victors of long-distance events during 1925. The chassis was orthodox, with pressed steel side-members, semi-elliptic springs in front and cantilevers behind until 1925. In 1926 the cantilevers gave place to double-shackled semi-elliptics and the 600 was renamed 630. The engine (cast-iron head, elektron block, aluminium crankcase) was coupled to a four-speed gearbox. Artillery or wire wheels were supplied according to coachwork.

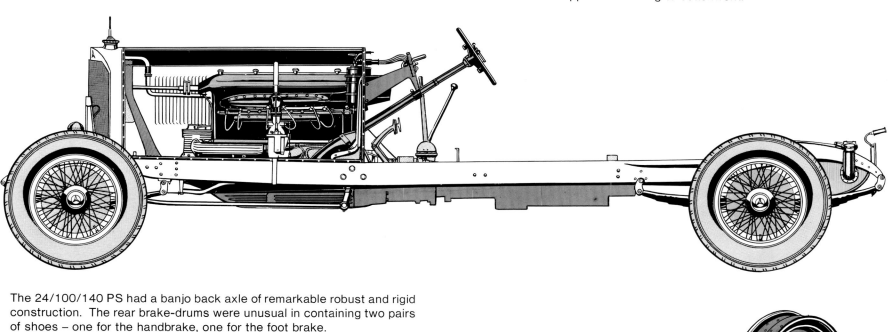

The 24/100/140 PS had a banjo back axle of remarkable robust and rigid construction. The rear brake-drums were unusual in containing two pairs of shoes – one for the handbrake, one for the foot brake.

21

The 2-litre cars which did so well in the 1924 Targa Florio took part in many ▷
subsequent German races. Here Otto Merz (14) and Karl Sailer (15) face
the starter in a handicap event at Solitude, 1924.

at Saalburg. Also in the awards list of the period we find the name of Rudolf Caracciola mentioned for the first time in connexion with Mercedes. Driving a 6/25/40 he came second in the 6 PS (i.e. 1^1/$_2$-litres) Class for Touring Cars in the Rastatt – Ettlingen race held during the Baden-Baden Motor Week 10 to 15 July 1923. Later the same year Caracciola collected several other trophies as a private entrant, for hill-climbs at Münnerstadt, Pforzheim, Solitude and Poehlberg. The previous year, while working as a salesman in the Daimler showrooms at Dresden, he had begun to make a name through racing Fafnir and Ego light cars as well as N.S.U. and Garelli motorcycles. Soon, after several successful drives in Works cars, he became an official team member. Rudolf Caracciola, greatest of all Mercedes drivers, was on his way.

The heavy supercharged 28/95 was at first reserved for Works drivers; then after winning the Targa Florio in 1922 it passed occasionally into the hands of private entrants, but it was never officially marketed. On the other hand smaller supercharged cars were made in limited numbers and sold to private individuals. During 1923 a batch of twenty-five two-seater sports cars was manufactured, based on the 6/25/40 but using the later 1500 cc engine. It was this new model, known as the 6/25/65, which brought success to Caracciola and Rosenberg in their early days. A similar batch of twenty-five racing cars was evolved by mounting the 2,612 cc four-cylinder engine from the 10/40/65 in the same 1^1/$_2$-litre chassis.

The fact that German participation in racing was once more allowed, at least in some countries, encouraged Mercedes to design a Grand Prix car for the international 2-litre formula due to be adopted in 1923, especially as the same cars would be eligible for the Indianapolis 500. By the autumn of 1922 their new four-cylinder supercharged engine was ready, with bore and stroke of 70 × 129, giving 1,989 cc. Twin overhead camshafts and 16 valves were used as on the

previous year's Targa Florio winner, but other details were taken from the smaller cars; the new 2-litre had its inlet valves on the left and exhaust valves on the right. The output exceeded 90 bhp. Various bodies were designed and built, including some streamlined, but the latter were not used for racing.

The four Indianapolis cars, shipped to the U.S. in April 1923, were two-seaters. The regulations no longer called for a riding mechanic (although Stuttgart preferred to provide one) and so the German cars looked very burly beside the slim American single-seaters. Of the four cars sent over three were to be driven by Lautenschlager, Sailer and Werner, with one work-horse in reserve. The best Mercedes time during practice was made by Werner, who qualified 15th, Lautenschlager being 17th and Sailer 20th. Sailer's fastest lap was 100 mph.

During the race it rained. Sailer lost control on the oily wet surface and smote the retaining wall. Both occupants were thrown out; the riding mechanic, Rieger, was seriously injured, but Sailer himself was able to continue, using the reserve car. Shortly afterwards Lautenschlager, too, crashed. 'The car was utterly uncontrollable', he said later, 'I was covered in oil from head to foot and I could hardly see... Suddenly I was thrown out, and came down God knows where.' Lautenschlager and his car retired, but the Germans were not the only entrants in trouble. Only three managed to complete the course without damage. In the final classification Sailer finished 8th and Werner 11th. The wrecked Mercedes were not shipped home; one of them was purchased by a German-American named Schmidt, who rebuilt it and ran it in the 1924 500 as a Schmidt Special. The remaining two cars were hurriedly modified at the Works with a view to running at Monza in the Italian Grand Prix. Unfortunately the political situation and Germany's galloping inflation obliged the Directors to cancel.

However, these preparations had not been wasted.

The ex-Crown Prince Wilhelm at the wheel of his Type 600 Mercedes in 1927. This model was sold in Britain as a 33/140 hp.

Mercedes 600 (24/100/140 PS, alias 33/140 hp), 1924 model, with open touring body. The 33 hp was the RAC rating.

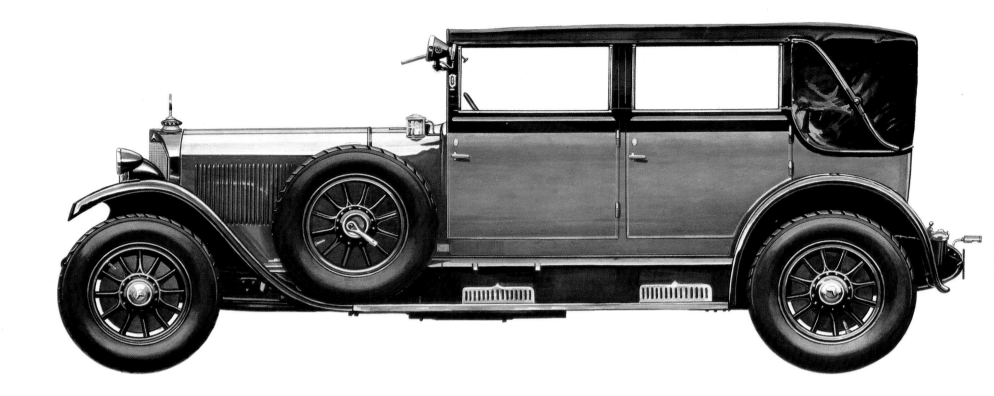

Although, like the Type 600, the 4-litre 15/70/100 or Type 400, carried the Porsche signature it could in no way be described as a sports car, either in appearance or performance. Carrying square-rigged saloon or (as above) All-weather bodywork, it could muster only 100 bhp to propel its weight of nearly 2¹/₂ tons (2400 kg) at 75 mph. The chassis and engine were similar to those of the 600 but on a smaller scale, with 3920 cc (80 × 130). The Type 400 was listed from 1924 (when the price was 20,000 Marks) until 1929, beside two sister supercharged Sixes, the 200 K and the 600s.

Included amongst the latter were several sporting models produced from 1927, of which the 24/110/160 or Type 630 K was undoubtedly the best known. 'The most marvellous car', as Raymond Mays called it, had an engine of similar dimensions to the standard Six, but could develop 160 bhp at 3100 rpm thanks to valves of larger diameter. Carrying fashionable coachwork – the car below is a two-seater coupé by Hibbard & Darrin – which set off the long bonnet and lagged exhaust pipes, 630 K Mercedes lived up to their reputation, easily attaining 90-95 mp.h.

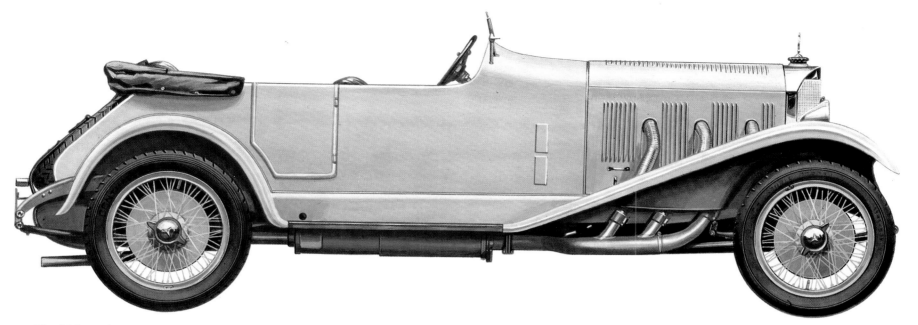

The 620, mechanically identical with the 630 K apart from being 2 in shorter in the wheelbase (11 ft instead of 11 ft 2) carried bodywork built at Sindelfingen which differed from it in various ways: large bonnet louvres, flared scuttle with separately folding two-piece windscreen, rear-mounted spare and long swept wings of determinedly sporting cut. Launched in 1927, it was built, in very small numbers, until 1932.

In the history of the supercharged Mercedes two models carried the designation 600 K: a short-chassis Type 600 (alias 24/100/140) and a very rare V-12 of which only twenty-three were built between 1938 and 1942. The best-looking, without question, was this coupé dating from 1938.

The 680 Ks, developed from the 24/100/140 short chassis, were competition cars pure and simple, handled only by works drivers. Their 6789 cc six-cylinder engines gave 130 bhp unblown, 180 with the blower engaged. Only six cars were made: two in 1927, four in 1928.

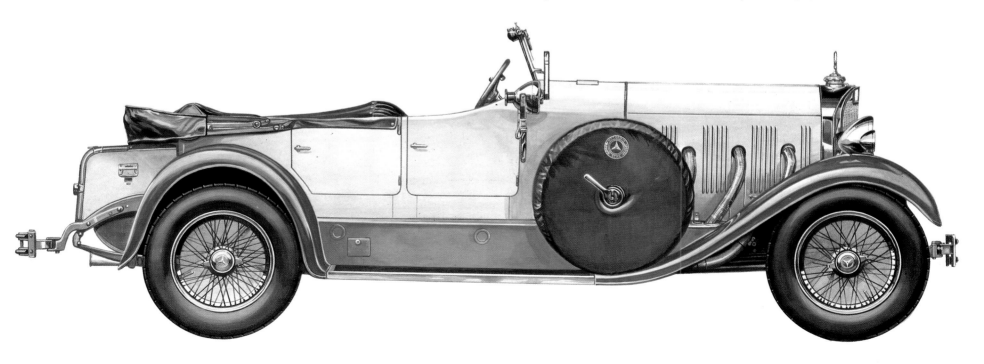

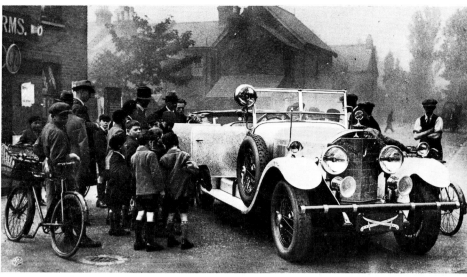

Doorless 'toast-rack' open tourers were popular with enthusiasts during the twenties. This is an early example of the short-chassis 620 K model of 1927. Jackie Coogan the boy film star poses in front of a 600 Mercedes limousine placed at his disposal by Daimler-Benz during a visit to Berlin in 1927. It was over 27 feet long and weighed 3 tons.

Very special was this Royal Mercedes, a 600 built for Abdul Aziz ibn Saud, King of the Hedjaz, and carrying his crossed-swords device on radiator cap and dumb-irons. The photograph was taken in London at the time of delivery. Mercedes 600 chassis on the importers' stand at the New York Motor Show ▷ in 1925. The artillery wheels suggest a limousine body.

The Indianapolis cars were entered for the 1924 Targa Florio, and by way of aperitif Otto Salzer used one of them to break the lap record for the Solitude circuit at 59.7 mph. In Sicily the cars were entrusted to Christian Werner, Christian Lautenschlager and one Alfred Neubauer, who later achieved fame as Team Manager to Mercedes-Benz. It proved to be Werner's day: he won the Targa Florio and the Coppa Florio as well. At least one of these cars survives, having been beautifully restored by the English engineer Gerald Palmer to compete in Vintage Sports-Car Club competitions.

Back, however, to 1924. The song of the 2-litre's blower was heard on many occasions: Otto Merz won the Klausen Pass hill-climb, Werner and Neubauer triumphed on the Semmering Pass, while the 1500s of Caracciola and Rosenberger won everything in the voiturette class. The year 1924 brought the Mercedes company 98 victories in the $1^{1}/_{2}$-and 2-litre classes.

Alfred Rosenberger and Rudolf Caracciola started their racing careers at almost the same moment – during the summer of 1923 – and during the next few seasons it was hard to say which of them was the more brilliant and successful. When, therefore, on 11 July 1926 Caracciola won his first German Grand Prix, driving at the Avus in the wet, his triumph was spoiled by the serious accident to Rosenberger. The two friends started side by side, and each was driving one of the new 130/150 straight eights placed at their disposal, strictly on loan, by the Mercedes factory. During practice, when the track was like a skating-rink, Caracciola quickly attained complete mastery of his powerful eight-cylinder. In the race itself he went on to win, although even so experienced a veteran as Jean Chassagne (Bugatti) slid off the track and crashed. Rosenberger, overcome by ether fumes from a leaking tank, skidded into a timing hut, injuring himself and his mechanic. Caracciola, who was a true amateur at the time, modestly disclaimed all credit for this first victory by the Daimler-Benz company, formed by the amalgamation of Mercedes and Benz only twelve

days before. It was all due to the car, Rudi said, to the help he had received all along the line, and to the impeccable team management of Neubauer and his mechanics. 'I just drove, that's all,' he said.

Here let us go back a little. In 1923 a new personality joined the Mercedes design team, namely Ferdinand Porsche. This remarkable engineer came from Austro-Daimler and was replacing Paul Daimler, who had left to join Horch, thus abandoning all hope of working on supercharged engines. As an early priority Porsche remodelled the victorious Targa Florio 'four'. By attention to the cylinder-head and valve-gear he extracted 150 bhp (with blower engaged) from this 2-litre without exceeding 4,800 revs.

Next, before starting on new designs he developed an amusing blown 'Special': this was a Targa Florio chassis in which he had installed a 1914 $4^{1}/_{2}$-litre Grand Prix engine. With it Otto Salzer knocked two seconds off the Semmering Pass hill-climb record which had stood at 7 m 7 s since 1909 – and this despite the fact that the blower gave out just before the start and had had to be replaced hurriedly by one taken from a standard blown 28/95. Another supercharged Mercedes, a 2-litre driven by Christian Werner, then promptly beat Salzer's time by 6 s.

Ferdinand Porsche was less fortunate with his first serious racing car. Taking as a basis designs drawn up by Paul Daimler two years before, the Austrian built a supercharged 2-litre engine with eight cylinders in line. This was the first eight-cylinder designed by Porsche and the first produced by Mercedes. The new car was to have made its debut at the Italian Grand Prix on 7 September 1924, but during the first few laps of practice, Christian Werner, the team manager, was plunged into deepest gloom. Clouds of steam were seen coming from under the bonnet. The bronze used for the heads was porous, and the engine was losing its water. Porsche ordered the cars back to Stuttgart. Since Fiat, too, had withdrawn several entries, the Italian G.P. promised to be a fiasco. The organisors dec-

German film star Hertha von Walter aboard her 1928 S. It was with open four-seater bodywork that these 36/220 hp Mercedes-Benz were most often seen, the majority built in the factory's own coachworks at Sindelfingen.

For some owners a 36/220 Mercedes S was merely a status symbol; others liked to enjoy its performance to the full. Actor Willy Fritsch was trying his on the Avus when he ran over a hen and nearly lost his windscreen.

At the inaugural race on the Nürburg Ring, on 19 June 1927, two Works 36/220 hp S Mercedes took part driven by Caracciola (1) and Rosenberger (2) plus the private 630 K of von Mosch (3). They finished first, second and third, to the great joy of some 500,000 spectators massed along the new 15½-mile circuit in the Eifel Mountains.

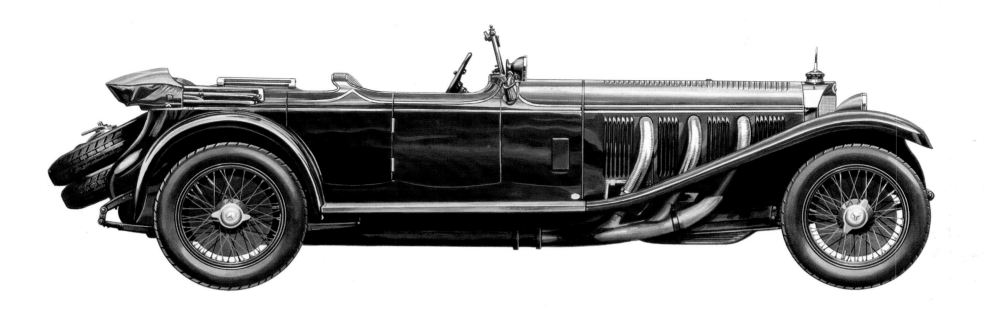

Direct descendants of the 680 K, the earliest S Mercedes – or 680 S –
retained the engine of that model but not the frame, for now an underslung
chassis was used, and the engine was moved 14 inches farther back, and
equipped with a low-mounted cooling fan. The radiator, lower than that of
the K cars, was recognisable because divided into seven by horizontal
bands. Of these 26/120/180 cars which can really be regarded as pre-pro-
duction models, only twenty were built in 1927 and six in 1928. Production
of 'standard' S models commenced in the spring of 1928, after important
changes in the engine-room: wet liners, bi-metal iron/aluminium pistons,
dual ignition with two plugs per cylinder, two updraught carburetters, bringing the output to 140 before the blower came in. Although designed primar-
ily for racing, the S sold also to wealthy enthusiasts for road use. Acceleration of 0-62 mph in 14 seconds and 105 mph maximum speed were out-
standing performances in those days. The model shown above, a close-
coupled four-seater is an SS – *Spezial-Sportwagen* – and is listed in the catalogue alongside two others: four-seater tourer and drophead coupé.

The SS (38/250 in Britain) differed from its predecessor the S (36/220 in
Britain) in having a higher elbow line, a radiator with eight horizontal mark-
ings and a more roomy interior. Beneath a bonnet pierced with two sets of
louvres was an engine of 100 mm bore instead of 98. Early examples (from
end of 1927 until March 1928) gave 140/200 hp, later ones (produced until
1930) 160/200 thanks to a slightly higher compression ratio. Bodies for
the 38/250 were built not only in Daimler's own shops at Sindelfingen, but
by many outside coachbuilders including Kellner, Neuss, Papler, Erdmann
& Rossi, Graber, Freestone & Webb, Martin Walter and Keibl, who built the
cabriolet opposite.

With an 11 ft 2 wheelbase and weighing 33 cwt (1650 kg) the SS chassis was of the underslung type, the frame being upswept at the back and the springs attached below the axle. Springing was semi-elliptic all round, with friction (Hartford type) shock-absorbers behind and Houdaille hydraulic dampers at the front. The massive back axle was stayed to the torque-tube; the gearbox had four forward speeds. Either 7.00-20 or 6.50-20 tyres were fitted. Brakes were more powerful, with one pair of shoes only in each of the finned brakedrums, the latter being coppered for better heat-dissipation. The bare chassis weighed 33 cwt, bodies varying from 181 kg – 400 pounds – for a two-seater to 680 kg (13 1/2 cwt) for the saloon.

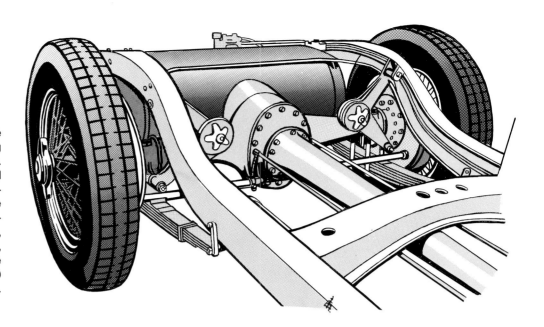

At the Barcelona International Exhibition of 1929, the SS or 38/250 hp Mercedes-Benz was introduced as 'the world's fastest sports car'. This was true enough, for the maximum speed was more than 110 mph.

Lilian Harvey, star of *Congress Dances* was as popular in Central Europe as she was in England. When summoned to Hollywood to make *My Lips Betray* for Fox Films she took with her this splendid 38/250 hp Mercedes SS, a 1932 Cabriolet C from Sindelfingen. The helmet wings, step instead of running-board, swiveling spotlamp and separate trunk are typical of the period.

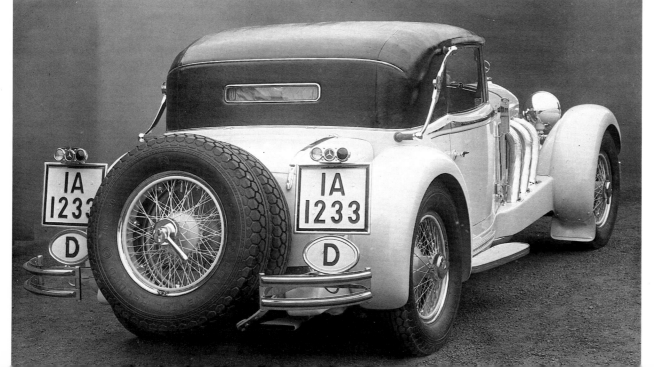

Perhaps there has never been a grander ▷ Motor Show exhibit than a 38/250 hp Mercedes in show-finished chassis form. All was stoved enamel, chromium plate and loving care: metal parts not enamelled or plated, such as rockerbox, carburetters, inlet manifolds and fan, were mottle finished by a cork and emery-powder.

In 1930 Rudolf Caracciola competed for the first time in the Mille Miglia, the 1000-mile open-road sports car race round Italy. With Christian Werner as riding mechanic he finished sixth, in a Mercedes-Benz SSK. Cars carried full touring equipment including hood, which is here being checked by scrutineers at Brescia prior to the start, while Caracciola stands by, in cloth cap, hands on hips. Werner is in white overalls.

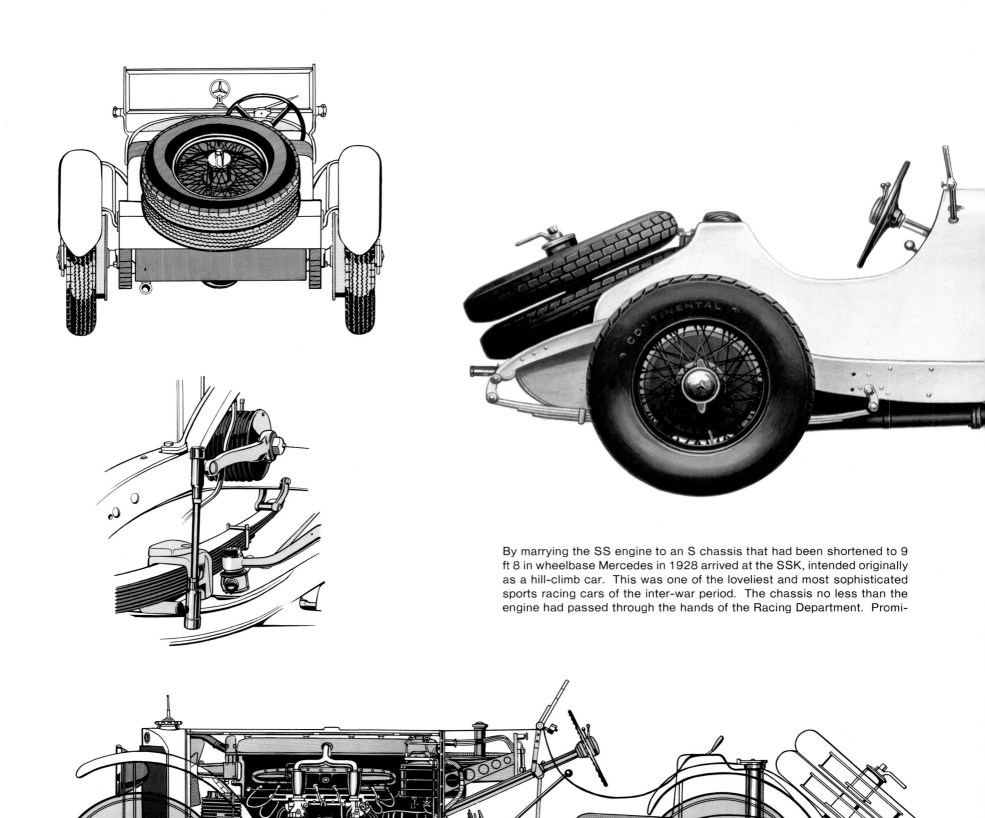

By marrying the SS engine to an S chassis that had been shortened to 9 ft 8 in wheelbase Mercedes in 1928 arrived at the SSK, intended originally as a hill-climb car. This was one of the loveliest and most sophisticated sports racing cars of the inter-war period. The chassis no less than the engine had passed through the hands of the Racing Department. Promi-

nent in this drawing are the Houdaille dampers, finned, like the brakedrums, blower and inlet manifold, for cooling. With a compression ratio of 5.75 : 1 the 7065 cc Six (100 × 150) delivered 220 bhp at 3300 rpm blown, 170 without supercharge. These quite respectable figures were considerably surpassed ty two Works racing cars, the 27/180/250 and the 27/300, in which latter machine the blower was permanent by engaged. The SSK was certainly no ordinary car as the following figures prove: 15 ft 4 over all, weight 34 cwt, 31-gallon (Imperial) fuel tank, 5¼ gallons of cooling water, nearly 2 gallons of oil in the sump, 11 mpg on petrol, 35 miles to the pint of oil and a top speed of 105 upwards depending on axle ratio.

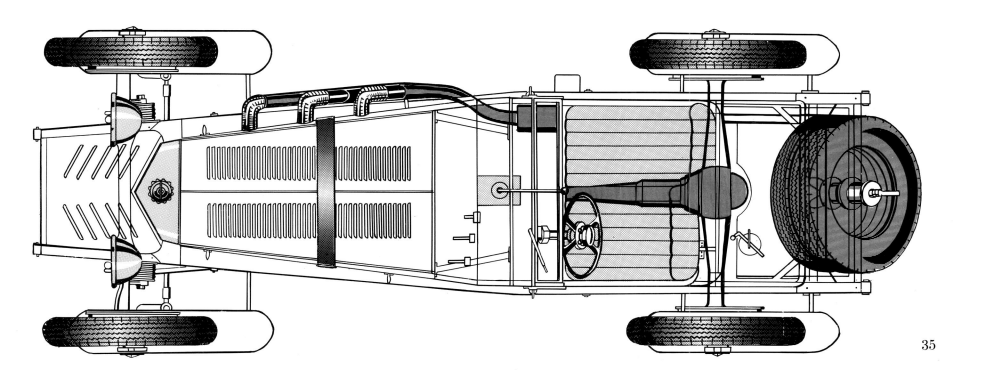

Caracciola became European Hill-climb Champion (sports cars) for the first time in 1930. This photograph taken at the Koenigsaal-Jilowischt event near Prague shows his SS cornering under complete control on the loose surface. Note the caps worn by driver and passenger.

Big long-distance road events are no nov- ▷
elty. Several were held in Germany between the wars. This one, starting from Baden-Baden, attracted an entry of 452, amongst them, naturally, an SSKL.
Manfred von Brauchitsh made his reputation by winning the *Avusrennen* in 1932 and by taking part in the motor-racing film *Kampf!* shortly afterwards. This full-length feature was directed by Eric Schönfelder for UFA Films. A camera man prepares to take action shots of the dashing young aristocrat in his SSKL.

In 1931 Carraciola again won the *Bergmeister* championship, sports car class. Daimler-Benz had withdrawn from racing, and so his SSKL (photographed at Koenigsaal) was officially his own property. The Mercedes team under Alfred Neubauer comprised 'Rudi' himself, his time-keeper wife Charly, Wilhelm Sebastian as co-driver and a mechanic, Zimmer.

Nicknamed 'Grandma' at the Works, this ▷
vintage 'special' using a 1922 Targa Florio chassis and a supercharged and modernised 1914 Grand Prix engine, was built at Untertürckheim for the Pforzheim enthusiast and businessman Adolf Rosenberger, who drove it in Continental events between 1927 and 1930. He is here seen winning the Racing class on the Klausen in 1928.

The 1931 hill-climb champion (Racing category) was Hans Stuck, known to British enthusiasts as holder of the Shelsley Walsh record. His privately owned SSKL (seen making fastest climb, racing car class, at Koenigsaal) was even more drastically lightened than Caracciola's.

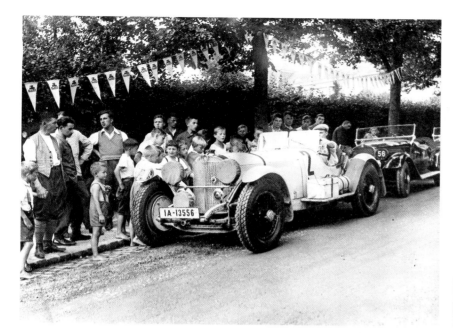

In 1931 Mercedes-Benz officially withdrew from racing. Paradoxically this retirement, brought about by the financial slump then prevailing in Germany, led eventually to the production of a purely racing Mercedes-Benz in which Rudolf Caracciola won his greatest victories during the *formule libre* period. At Alfred Neubauer's instigation the company agreed to sell Caracciola a specially modified SSK, to lend him two of their best racing mechanics, and to pay the expenses of this much reduced team. Working directly under Hans Nibel, the Chief Designer, two development engineers, Max Wagner and Fritz Nallinger subjected an SSK chassis to a drastic slimming cure. Putting holes wherever possible in frame, cross-members, dash, brackets, and so on, they pared away more than 270 pounds. They raised the output to 240/300 bhp, thanks partly to a blower of larger capacity than those on the Works SSK. An extra oil tank was installed in the scuttle, and the fuel lines were duplicated. It was in this SSKL (*L* signifying *leicht,* German for lightweight) Caracciola won the 1931 Mille Miglia in April 1931. For this 1000-miles race over public roads the car was fitted with three large lamps; it carried also a toolbox and a spare fuel can. Six other SSKs received the SSKL treatment during 1931. Acquired by firstclass drivers like Hans Stuck and Manfred von Brauchitsch they shone both in circuit racing and hill-climbs until 1933. Of all supercharged Mercedes and Mercedes-Benz cars those of the S series are the rarest because Daimler-Benz built only 149 of the S, 114 SS, 31 modified SSK and 7 of the SSKL.

Two SSKL chassis were fitted with single-seater streamline bodywork. The first of these (above) was the lightened version with which Manfred von Brauchitsch campaigned during and after 1930. The body was designed by an aeronautical engineer, Reinhard von Koenig-Fachsenfeld, built in the Vetter shops at Cannstatt and entered by von Brauchitsch for the 183-mile *Avusrennen* in 1932 at the Avus track. Nicknamed 'the Zeppelin on Wheels' it had no difficulty in winning, at an average of 120 mph, which was 5½ mph faster than Caracciola's speed the previous year in a standard SSKL. The other car (left) was built by the Works for the 1933 Avus race. Not com-

pleted until the evening before practice, it was driven through the night, from Stuttgart to Berlin, without lights, by Otto Merz. The weather turned wet next morning, and on his first practice lap Merz lost control on the slippery *pavé* surface, crashed and was killed. Later that day von Brauchitsch driving the other streamliner faced the starter in the hope of repeating his previous victory; but repeated wheel-changes slowed him and he had to be content with sixth place. It is interesting to note the likeness between the body of the 1933 Works streamliner (left) and these of the 1934 '750 kg' Grand Prix cars.

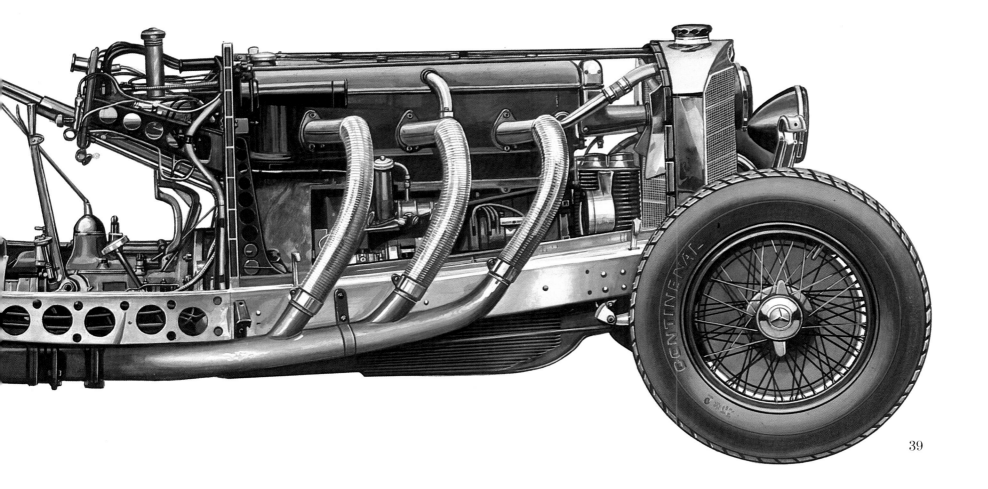

Mercedes figured six times amongst the winners of the Klausen Pass hill-climb, held on eleven occasions from 1922 to 1934 in Central Switzerland. The course was 13 miles long and rose to a height of 6,500 feet. In 1927 Caracciola in a Mercedes S (above, left) won the Sports category and broke the record in 17m 35.4s. Five years later Hans Stuck, driving an SSKL (below, left) improved this to 17m 0.50s.

ided therefore to postpone the event for five weeks, and Porsche found time to design a new head. By race day, 19 October, the situation was little improved. The four Mercedes entrusted to Werner, Masetti, Neubauer and Count Louis Zborowski proved almost undriveable because they oversteered so much; they also suffered from bad brakes and clutch trouble. Two hours were spent trying to start the Werner and Zborowski cars. Sparking-plugs were changed again and again – always a different cylinder – which meant trying each in turn while they were burning hot. Eventually all four cars reached the grid. But on the 43rd lap Masetti stopped with a broken fuel pipe and on the 44th Zborowski met with a fatal accident. The remaining two cars were withdrawn. Porsche's straight-eight had got off to a bad start.

At Stuttgart, however, they refused to give up. The cars were completely redesigned – successfully, so that efforts to make the 130/150 hp cars worthy of men like Merz, Werner and Caracciola finally paid off. In twenty-seven starts the model was placed twenty-one times, including Caracciola's 1926 German G.P. already noted.

We must now pause to enquire how it was that Mercedes put so much effort into developing supercharged engines when they had never any intention of putting them into production cars. All this, moreover, while the motoring papers ran articles reminding manufacturers that the saying 'The racing car of today is the touring car of tomorrow' had largely lost its point now that the majority of races no longer took place on ordinary roads but on specially built circuits, and that so far as racing cars were concerned technical research was gradually giving place to sensationalism.

It must be conceded that the Mercedes operation in Stuttgart was headed by men who knew precisely for what reasons they authorised such heavy investment in a supercharged car at a time when the majority of Mercedes manufactured were orthodox unblown four-cylinder and six-cylinder side-valves. Nowadays we should describe the technical men in charge from 1923 to 1925 – Ernst Berge, Josef Brecht, Hermann Gross, Wilhelm Kissel, Richard Lang, Ferdinand Porsche, Friedrich Nallinger and Carl Schippert to name but a few – as experts in marketing. Their strategy was to see that glamorous, important and newsworthy figures were kept supplied with glamorous, fierce and newsworthy supercharged cars, thus whipping up enthusiasm amongst the mass of ordinary buyers. The new Managing Director, Dr Wilhelm Kissel, who took office in June 1926, regarded supercharged cars as splendid publicity. Models built at his instigation during the late twenties and early thirties earned Mercedes-Benz world-wide acclaim. The fact that supercharged Mercedes existed, as well as workaday road-going vehicles had a considerable effect on the Company's balance sheet. What manufacturer during the twenties – with the exception perhaps of Rolls Royce – could afford to stand aloof from racing when every victory added to the lustre to the ordinary Mercedes range? And once having taken a hand, surely one should try and hold all the trumps...

Supercharged engines for ordinary standard cars were and remained the exception, not only because of the cost of production and higher selling price but also because in the early years at least the public remained sceptical. 'Supercharged engines are less reliable... one could get the same extra power by raising the compression ratio... modern engines are quite powerful enough without supercharging...' So ran the usual arguments. In 1925 it was too soon to prove or disprove questions of longevity, for supercharged engines had not been around long enough. 'We make due allowance for the extra stresses undergone by these engines', said the management in the spring of 1925, replying to certain criticisms, and again 'It would be hardly flattering to our engineers to suggest that they were incapable of developing one compo-

On the colossal *Grosser Mercedes* the supercharger proved not only desirable but essential because limousines of the 1930-1938 770 K series like this one weighed 54 cwt. The engine marked several departures from Mercedes practice: it was a straight eight instead of a six, and the valves were operated by pushrods and rockers instead of an overhead camshaft. With bore and stroke 95 × 135 this imposing 7655 cc motor claimed 150 bhp unblown but would put out 200 bhp at 2800 with the supercharger engaged. These early cars had semi-elliptic springs. In 1933 the gearbox had 4 forward speeds; in 1938 it had 5. Between 1938 and 1942 Mercedes-Benz produced a small number of more powerful cars, also called 770, giving 230 bhp at 3200 rpm and said to be capable of 105 mph. These cars had new lower chassis fabricated from oval-section tubes, independant suspension at the front and a De Dion back axle. The five-speed gearbox had syncromesh on all ratios.

In 1933 a new supercharged model was added to the Mercedes range which, apart from the 770 supercharged straight eight, comprised rather dull side-valve machines: Types 170, 370 *Mannheim* (inherited from Benz), 200 and 290, all unblown. The new Type 380 (alias 15/90/120) had a pushrod o.h.v. straight-eight engine similar in design to the 770, of 3820 cc (78 × 100). Announced at the 1933 Berlin motor show the 380 was a low-built car for its day and modern in having independent suspension for all four wheels, allied to a rigid chassis of partially boxed construction. Two lengths of wheelbase were offered, 10 ft 6 and 10 ft 3$\frac{1}{2}$, the short-chassis cars having rather more power (140 bhp at 3600 rpm) and a top speed of 100 mph, with acceleration from 0 to 62 mph in 22 seconds. A gearbox with six forward speeds was fitted. Seven types of body were available on Type 380 K (15/90/140): saloon, drophead cabriolets A, B (right), C and D; open two-seater and open four-seater. The price was the same for all models.

The 380 was much praised for its comfort and road-holding; it was indeed very modern in design and strikingly good on the rough roads of the period. Rear suspension was by coil springs and swinging half axles, at the front by coil springs and wishbones (right) the first time these had been used on a car of this size.

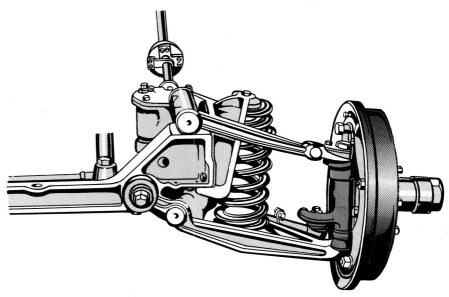

Passenger's view of a Mercedes 380 Cabriolet A of 1934, complete with opening windscreen, sun visor, horn-ring, cigar-lighter and glove-compartments flanking the fascia panel. Instruments include fuel-gauge, oil-pressure gauge, ammeter, rev-counter, speedometer and clock.

Most of the 380s and 380 Ks had convertible bodies of one sort or another, for two, three or five persons. This 1933 four-door owner-driver saloon is an exception. The coachwork is by Baur of Stuttgart.

Grosser Mercedes models were favourite cars for State and ceremonial occasions in Germany, during both the Weimar Republic and the Third Reich. The upper photograph opposite shows Hitler at the opening of a new Autobahn; below, Goering and Roehm are seen leading a Nazi procession through the Brandeburg Gate, Berlin, in 1933 soon after the Nazis came to power.

This 1931 770 K has landaulet cabriolet de ville coachwork by Baur of Stuttgart. The 770 and 770 K Mercedes certainly earned their name *Grosser Mercedes*. Powered by a supercharged 7.6-straight-eight they turned the scale at nearly 3 tons – and considerably more when armour-plated and fitted with bullet-proof glass.

nent invention without detracting from the virtues of the whole.' They emphasised that the supercharger was there to give power in reserve, for reaching maximum speed, climbing hills or overtaking on the road or racing circuit. 'The possibility of making better use of the power available at all times definitely increases... reliability', the Company announced.

It was as true in the 1920s as it is today that the compression ratio of normally aspirated engines cannot be increased at will, contrary to what opponents of supercharging claimed. In those days a ration of 6:1 was quite as high as one could go on ordinary petrol without risk of detonation; high-compression engines were apt to be harsh, hard to start and critical as to sparking plugs. Another advantage, ran the Mercedes argument, was that supercharged engines were lighter because, to obtain 100 bhp, say, an unblown engine would have to be larger; it would take more material and therefore weigh more; and weight-saving was what sports cars were all about...

As from 1923 the development of new models had been the concern of Ferdinand Porsche. Besides the racing cars already mentioned he had new supercharged models ready by 1924. These models had the usual three-number description, first the PS (German fiscal horsepower at 4 PS to the litre), then the power claimed with and without supercharge. There was an 8/40/60 2-litre known also as Model 200 and 200 K which launched the Mercedes habit of using hundreds to denote litres which continues to this day. The 'K' stood not for *Kompressor* but for *kurz* – or short chassis model. This 200 series was a six-cylinder side-valve of 1988 cc (65 × 100) running at 5.6:1 compression ratio. It was usually fitted with four-(K) or six-seater closed bodywork and weighed about 30 cwt. Tests dated November 1924 give a top speed of 71 mph. Simultaneously with the Type 200 appeared Type 600, a vast overhead-camshaft Six of more than 6 litres (94 × 150, 6240 cc) called also 24/100/140*. The 140 bhp blown were delivered at 3,200 rpm and a top speed of

77 mph was quoted. Six types of body were shown including a Pullman Limousine on a 12 ft 6 in wheelbase. Alternative axle ratios were 4:1 and 4.76:1.

Finally a third new model came out that year. This was the Type 400 alias 15/70/100 overhead-camshaft six, cylinder dimensions 80 × 130, 3920 cc. This model was known in Britain as the 24/100 hp, from its 24 hp RAC rating. It was listed also in 1926, 1927 and 1928, becoming known in 1928 as the 4-litre. Externally the six-cylinder cars could be recognised by their longer bonnets but the chassis layout was similar to that of the fours: pressed-steel side-members, semi-elliptic springs at the front, cantilever springs behind and mechanically operated four-wheel brakes as on the rest of the Mercedes range. During its first season Max Sailer drove a 15/70/100 down to Sicily on a sporting reconnaissance. The machine behaved very well and was to remain in the German catalogue until 1929, two years longer than the 8/40/60.

The 24/100/140 (33/140 hp) on the other hand was to sire a famous line, and to win no fewer than twenty-seven events during 1925. This success continued during the ensuing two seasons, while the old 28/95 and the four-cylinder blown cars also finished well.

The great thing about these supercharged Mercedes was that they could be bought, giving the private owner a chance to enter for races and sprints and hill climbs of the period. In 1924 a two-seater 10/40/65 cost 19,500 Marks, a 15/70/100 cost 500 Marks more. Prices for the big 24/100/140 ranged from 23,000 to more than 30,000 depending on coachwork, which was almost twice as much as an eight-cylinder Horch, one of Germany's luxury cars. Only the noble Maybach cost more than a supercharged Mercedes.

The 'working agreement' reached in 1924 between the Daimler Motoren Gesellschaft and Benz & Cie of Mannheim led in 1926 to a merger of the two companies, the laurel-wreath badge of Benz being combined with a Mercedes three-pointed star to form the trademark of the new company, Mercedes-Benz.

* Listed in Britain as the 33/140 hp, the RAC rating being 33 hp.

This 1930 770 K seven-seater Limousine has coachwork from the Sindelfingen shops belonging to Daimler-Benz.

Type 770 K *Grosser Mercedes* chassis became lower over the years. This is a 1935 Cabriolet F, with windscreen defroster.

The ex-Regent of Hungary, Field-Marshal the Archduke Joseph of Austria poses beside a 1933 *Grosser Mercedes* at Budapest. This form of All-Weather body was called a Cabriolet D.

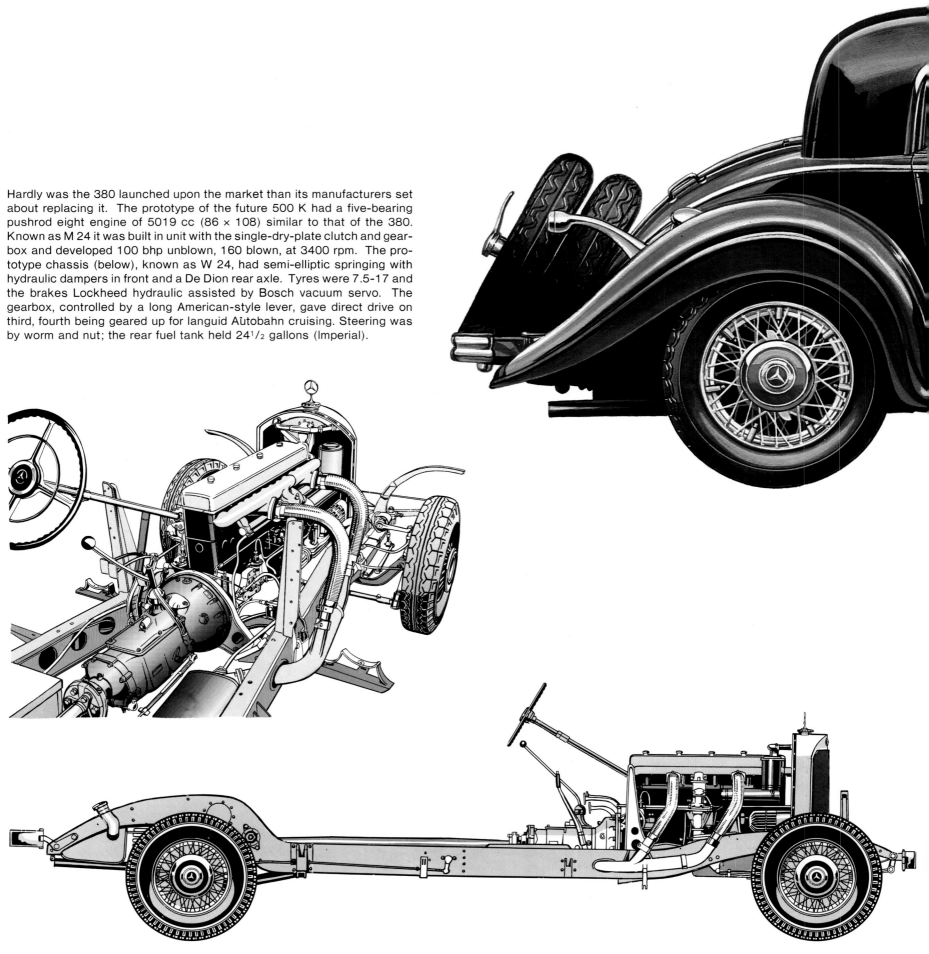

Hardly was the 380 launched upon the market than its manufacturers set about replacing it. The prototype of the future 500 K had a five-bearing pushrod eight engine of 5019 cc (86 × 108) similar to that of the 380. Known as M 24 it was built in unit with the single-dry-plate clutch and gearbox and developed 100 bhp unblown, 160 blown, at 3400 rpm. The prototype chassis (below), known as W 24, had semi-elliptic springing with hydraulic dampers in front and a De Dion rear axle. Tyres were 7.5-17 and the brakes Lockheed hydraulic assisted by Bosch vacuum servo. The gearbox, controlled by a long American-style lever, gave direct drive on third, fourth being geared up for languid Autobahn cruising. Steering was by worm and nut; the rear fuel tank held 24$\frac{1}{2}$ gallons (Imperial).

The running-gear was greatly changed, two. The front end received the now fashionable independant suspension without which no Continental car of its day was complete, the system comprising coil springs and wishbones as on the 380; but for reasons of commercial policy the prototype's De Dion rear end was replaced by 'swing axle' and duplicated coil springs. Tyres of 6.5 in section replaced the 7.00-17. To the six body styles formerly listed for the 380 there was added a streamlined two-seater coupé called an *Autobahn-Kurier* – Motorway Express. All standard bodies were made at Sindelfingen and all models carried the same price-tag: 22,000 Marks. For customers requiring something more exclusive there were special bodies like the 1935 coupé shown above. Two-seaters, fixed-head and drophead coupé were normally built upon a 9 ft 9 in wheelbase and weighed 47 cwt; saloons had a 10 ft 9½ in chassis and averaged 50 cwt. The 500 K short cars would do 100 mph; petrol consumption was about 8 mpg.

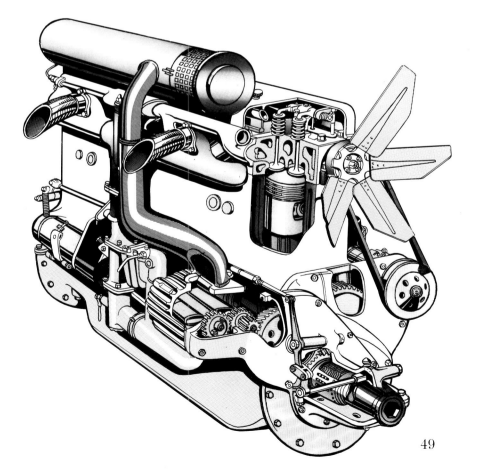

A number of changes were made to the prototype 500 engine, M 24 (opposite page) in course of developing the version fitted as standard. The latter, known as M 24/I is shown (right). Both engines used a straight-eight monobloc casting and vertical o.h.v. It will be noticed that the small vertical air-filter (beside the fan) deemed sufficient at first gave way on production cars to a huge horizontal air-cleaner silencer, to make room for which it was necessary to reverse the positions of the inlet and exhaust manifolds. The cut-away drawing reveals the smallness of the valves on these 5-litre cars; it also shows the blower-drive gears and the linkage and multi-disc clutch by which the supercharger was brought into engagement. The small size of the blower will be noted, also the absence of fins leading to the pressurised updraught carburetter. The chromium-plated flexible outside exhaust pipes were a tremendous piece of salesmanship.

'The most marvellous car'

The first supercharged car to bear the new combine's name Mercedes-Benz was a model coded 12/60/90 or Type 300. Little is known about this except that it was an eight-cylinder 3-litre (67 × 105, 2960 cc) and that it never went beyond the experimental stage. Instead Porsche and his engineers set about making what Bentleys might have called a Speed Model from the ordinary big six 24/100/140. This 600 K sports model appeared in 1927, with wheelbase shortened by 14 inches to 3400 mm (11 ft 2 in) with shorter, more compact body, weight reduced by at least 4 cwt and axle-ratios to suit a sporting career. It was sold in England as the 33/180 hp.

The 600 K bore the unmistakeable stamp of Ferdinand Porsche, who remained with Mercedes-Benz until the end of 1927 before leaving to join the Steyr company in Austria, where he remained only a short time before returning to Stuttgart and opening a research establishment of his own.

Several variants of the 24/100/140 were constructed: a 24/110/160, sold as Type 620 and 620 K, a 24/100/140 listed as Type 630; a 25/130/220 racing car also called 660 K and two type 680 K, in 26/130/180 and 26/145/270 guise, also for racing.

Even though all these models, irrespective of whether limousine, *grande routière* or 'super sports' are today indistinguishably known under the letter K, they were by no means all of a feather. The most widely sold Type K was the 630 K 24/100/160 bearing the works code W 9456 which corresponded, apart from the wheelbase and tyre size, to the 620 24/110/160.

The English journalist Edgar N. Duffield, editor of *The Auto,* made a comparative road test between a 630 K and the big 40 CV Renault, in the course of which the Mercedes lapped Brooklands track at 85 mph. He particularly liked the tyre-inflation compressor supplied as standard, the two-tone horn and the flexibility of the 6.3 litre engine. Only the heaviness of the clutch seemed to trouble the test driver; Raymond Mays, however, then at the peak of his fame as a hill-

climb driver, described it as 'the most marvellous car'.

An outward and very visible sign of the supercharger, used from the earliest K type 3, were the flexible exhaust pipes issuing from the bonnet, a feature which coachbuilders quickly turned to advantage, and set off by means of swept wings and wide running-boards − although the outside pipes were in fact strictly functional, being there to convey heat from under the bonnet. The K had a top speed, guaranteed by the company, of 90 mph, which made it the fastest standard model of its day. The experimental 26/130/180, which was similar to the 630 K except for its capacity of 6.8 litres (98 bore instead of 94 mm) and lightened chassis would easily exceed 100 mph. Special versions like the 25/130/220 660 K and 26/145/270 680 K reached almost 110 mph (170 kph +) but these remained purely experimental and were never raced. Their underslung chassis made them the direct forerunners of the SSK and SSKL, of which more later. Of the 660 K, only ten were built in 1927, eleven in 1928, five in 1929 and one, the last, in 1930. Many different gearbox and axle ratios were used. According to a test report of 15 March 1929, the model suffered from inadequate oil cooling. A few examples were fitted with special coachwork by Vanden Plas and others in the course of aerodynamic experiments. One example is said to have been supplied to special order as late as 1933.

Production of the 680 K was even more restricted. Two examples were built in 1927, four in 1928 and one engine alone, of 6830 cc, with bore and stroke 100 × 150. A final drive ratio of 2.4:1 allowed this 1620 kg ($32^1/_2$ cwt) two-seater to reach 110 mph.

Although the K type earned the respect of its rivals and was much appreciated by private enthusiasts both in racing and on the road, there were demands early in 1927 for still more powerful and lighter machines. There was no question of withdrawing the K, but rather of forcing Messrs Kissel, Nallinger and Porsche to augment the Mercedes range by a more highly developed sports car. Thus was inaugurated the S series, of which the first model was the 680 S or 26/120/180, which in its original form bore the code number 9856. This six-cylinder 6.8-litre appeared in 1927, when twenty were made, with a further six in 1928. With the short 3400 mm (11 ft 2 in) wheelbase characteristic of the K types and a weight of only 1680 kilos (33 cwt) the 680 S could attain exactly 178 kph (110 mph). The price was 26,000 Marks. Shortly afterwards, in the spring of 1928 Mercedes-Benz brought out the 26/140/180.

The engine of this new 680 S differed in several respects from that of the 680 K and the earlier 680 S. The 150 mm stroke remained unchanged but the bore was now 98 mm, giving 6789 cc, and the block now had wet liners and there were two updraught pressure carburetters. Compression ratio was raised to 5:1, bringing an extra 20 bhp at 3,400 rpm; top speed was now about 115 mph (185 kph).

Only two examples of this 680 S were made, essentially experimental cars from which production S cars and their derivative the SS were worked up. One of them received the first dual-ignition head, with two sparking plugs per cylinder, the inlet side being fired by magneto (Bosch M 180/7 plugs) the exhaust side by coil (Bosch DM 220/5 plugs).

This engine marked the adoption of a new form of numbering by Mercedes: it was known as M 06 (M for *Motor*) and its chassis as W 06 (W for *Wagen*). Like its predecessor this engine was a single-ohc six, with Elektron cylinder block and cast-iron head.

Before manufacture of production 680 S cars began in 1928, some further changes were made: bi-metallic iron and alluminium pistons were fitted, nickel-chrome steel con-rods and a hollow-forged four-bearing crankshaft with vibration-damper. Competition cars had a supplementary oil tank mounted on the bulkhead, the two gallons in the sump being deemed insufficient. In actual fact the allowance proved to be on the generous side and although this was no disadvantage for competition work, there was a tendency when driving slowly in traffic for the plugs to oil up.

The W 06 chassis, known in Britain as the S or 36/220 hp, was of the underslung type, that is the rear springs passed under the axle instead of above as in the K or 33/180 hp. The engine was mounted 14 inches further back in the chassis, as was the radiator, and there were louvres in the bonnet; the gear-driven cooling fan came lower than that of the K. The 680 S – or to use the popular British name, 36/220 – Mercedes, offered with a choice of axle ratios (2.48, 2.5, 2.75 and 3:1) was suited to almost all forms of competition. The sports four-seater weighed $34\frac{1}{2}$ cwt (1720 kilos), although as a two-seater *Spezial-Sportwagen* it was somewhat lighter. The Spezial-Sportwagen came also as a drophead coupé in Germany, and in England too to special order. This model was timed at 177.6 kph (110 mph) thus breaking the German record for sports-cars, although this was really beside the point because the list of records broken throughout Europe grew longer day by day. In the autumn of 1930 the Italian driver F. Calfisch set a new record for the flying kilometre between Giubiasco and Cadenazzo in Switzerland at 191.5 kph (nearly 118 mph). Calfisch, a Neapolitan businessman, had been driving as a works-sponsored private owner for Mercedes since 1924, and with almost as many wins to his credit as men like Otto Merz and Christian Werner.

The 680 S was always thought of as a racing car, although less ambitious customers – corresponding to people who in the past had run a 33/180 – used them for everyday running or as touring cars. Of the W 06 chassis 149 were built, including six very stark 26/190/250 two-seaters produced in 1929 and capable of nearly 125 mph.

Naturally the 680 S was fitted with a Roots blower. This supercharger was driven at 2.6 times crankshaft speed and was engaged by means of a 22-disc clutch engaging a gear on the end of the blower shaft. If it was intended to keep the blower engaged for any

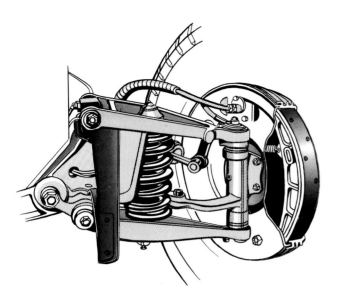

On the 500 and 540 series the wishbone assembly was mounted upon a vertical pivot; the road wheel and supension members therefore had a small amount of fore-and-aft float, restrained by a 'kick shackle' bolted to the cross member. Similar arrangements were used on the 1938-39 Grand Prix cars. This drawing shows the i.f.s. on a 540 K, the large brake-shoes and finned drums. Rear suspension was by coil springs and swing axles.

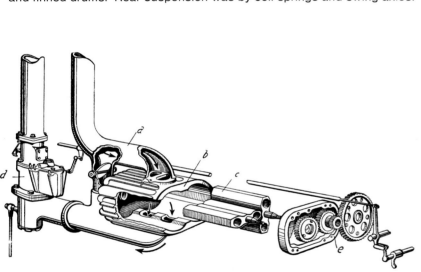

The supercharger on the 540 K was of course a Roots blower. When the driver pressed his accelerator beyond its normal travel a clutch brought the supercharger into operation and at the same time closed the atmospheric intake on the carburetter. Driven by gearing (e) from the nose of the crankshaft, a pair of lobes or paddles (c) rotated within the blower casing (d) compressing pure air drawn in via duct (a) from an air-cleaner/silencer and forcing it through ducts (see arrows) under pressure to the carburetter (d). Some engines had a small vertical air-filter/silencer mounted on the blower casing (below, left), with finned delivery pipe; others drew their air from a large horizontal air-cleaner/silencer above the inlet and exhaust manifolds.

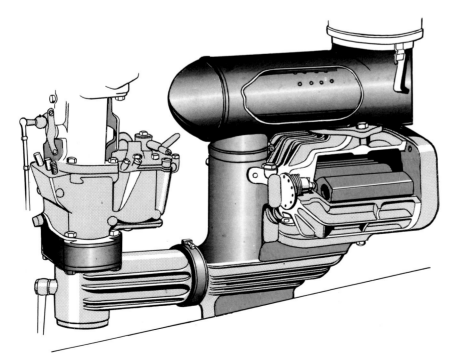

The 540 K, if one excepts one or two experimental cars derived from it, and the shortlived 600 K (see page 25) was the last production supercharged Mercedes; and the most popular, 409 being built: 97 in 1936, 145 in 1937, 95 in 1938 and 69 in 1939. It was also the most refined and the best looking – especially the sports two-seater (above). Even today these cars continue to enchant us by the harmony of their lines, despite their exaggeration. Perhaps if called upon to drive them in modern traffic we might modify our opinions; yet on motorways they would shine: cruising quietly and luxuriously at 85 mph except when the silence is rent by the blare of the supercharger as the driver puts his foot down and winds the car up past 'the ton'. The 540 Ks owed their performance to their straight-eight engine of 5401 cc (88 × 111) which developed 115/180 at 3400 rpm. Although there existed two lengths of wheelbase, 10 ft 9½ for saloons and 9 ft 9½ for most two-seaters and coupés, the letter *K* did not mean 'short' (German *kurz*) as hitherto. It now stood for *Kompressor,* i.e. supercharger. Besides, after 1938 the 540 K was available only on the short wheelbase. The following styles were listed: roadster (open two-seater), cabriolets A, B, and C, drophead coupé (recognisable by the *absence* of hoodirons), four-seater tourer (below, left), *Kombinationswagen* with hard-top, close-coupled two-door saloon. All, except roadster and tourer came complete with suitcases tailored to fit, as may be seen in the coupé below. Openable cars had leather upholstery, closed models cloth. Four-seaters had reclining seats.

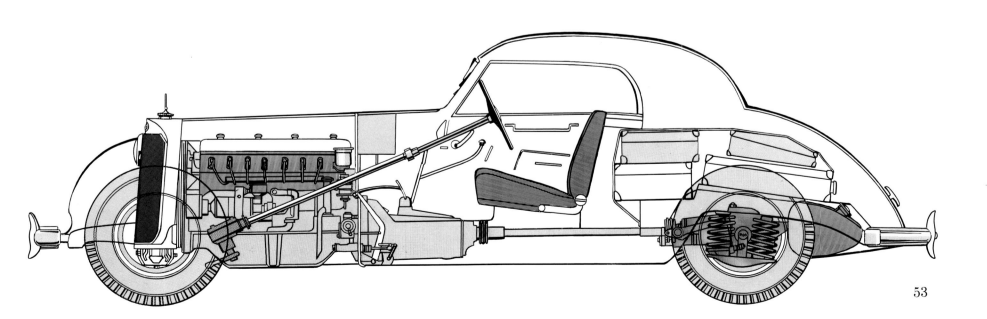

53

At the 1939 Berlin Motor Show Daimler-Benz introduced the 580 K Mercedes as replacement for the 540 K upon which it was based. In fact only twelve of these 5.8-litre straight eights were built: ten in 1939 and two in 1940. None was ever sold to the public.

Big supercharged Mercedes always attract attention. In this picture a 500 K forges through the crowds outside the Radio Exhibition in Berlin before the war.

The famous *Autobahn-Kurier* 500 K of 1934 set a fashion: this streamlined 540 K was built at Sindelfingen for a private customer. It has a steel sunshine roof.

540 K 'Cabriolet B' from Sindelfingen. 'Cabriolet B' meant a four-light four-seater all-weather body. The rubberised mohair top folded right back, but the sides remained standing. Spare wheels were carried in the wings, and the boot contained a pair of fitted suitcases, supplied with the car.

Only details such as the rear-lamp clusters, bumpers and spare-wheel cover betray the period when this 540 K body was built. This splendid coupé dates only from 1950; it is by the German coachbuilder Hebmüller.

length of time or to use it repeatedly customers were recommended to fit specially 'hard' heat-resisting sparking-plugs and to run on a mixture of petrol and benzole. A second 8-disc clutch acted upon the blower on the overrun.

The banjo back axle – in which the differential casing was integral with the torque-tube – was an innovation. Gearbox ratios (3:1, 1.81:1, 1.21:1) were higher than on the 33/180 Model K and the mechanically operated leading-shoe brakes more powerful. A few S cars were fitted with a Bosch vacuum servo.

So far as damping was concerned, Stuttgart clung to conventional solutions as used on the Mercedes which won the French Grand Prix in 1908: production cars had friction shock-absorbers at the rear, and Houdaille hydraulic dampers at the front.

Models S and K had the same 11 ft 2 in (3400 mm) wheelbase, although the two chassis differed in weight – 30 cwt (1500 kilos) for the K, 26 cwt (1300 kilos) for the S. On the latter model tuning experts had managed to extract 280 bhp, enabling it to reach 125 mph. This magic figure in Britain and America, and the equally magic 200 kph made the 36/220 S the dream car of every enthusiast.

Rudolf Caracciola showed off the S in particularly brilliant fashion. On 26 June 1927, during the inaugural race at the Nürburg Ring, he made best time of the day over twelve laps of the North and South loops of the new circuit, and his speed of 63.5 mph (101.1 kph) was far far better than the 92.5 kph of Christian Werner, winner of the racing classes in a supercharged 2-litre. Adolf Rosenberger came second in another 36/220 and Momberger was third, in a 33/180. The 1927 season brought great success to both these models. Caracciola, Willy Walb and von Mosch in particular shone in the various speed events during the Baden-Baden motor week, while Merz, Werner and Walb finished first, second and third in

the German Grand Prix on 17 July, held for the first time at the Nürburg Ring.

It was at this meeting that Daimler-Benz painted a red stripe on the bonnet of their racing cars so that spectators could recognise them from a distance. It was also in an S (but fitted with a 38/250 SS engine) that Caracciola won the 1929 RAC Tourist Trophy race on the Newtonards Circuit in Northern Ireland. In 1931 private owners Prince Djordjadze and Goffredo Zehender came first in the 24-Hours of Spa-Francorchamps in Belgium, and the Ivanowski/Stoffel partnership came an honourable second at Le Mans. During the 1928 season alone the 36/220 marked up fifty-three wins and set seventeen records.

That was the season which saw the debut of the Mercedes-Benz SS, or 38/250 as it was called in the English-speaking countries. This model, like its predecessors, was produced in a number of different versions which must not be confused. The earliest type was on sale from the end of 1927 until March 1928 as Model 700 and figured in the German catalogue as a 27/140/200.

That series comprised only thirteen cars. The final version of the SS was catalogued under the name 27/160/200 or Model 710. Within the factory these two were known respectively as W 1156 and W 1156 SII. Examples of the 710 delivered after March had an engine capacity of 7065 cc to bring it within a new tax classification, but by raising the compression ratio from 5:1 to 5.2:1 maximum horsepower unblown rose from 140 to 160 bhp. The chassis too underwent modification. Better to satisfy customers' requirements the factory made increasing use of outside coachbuilders. A number of high-performance coupé and saloon bodies were built, handsome but often absurdly heavy. Amongst the most popular were the names of Kellner, Neuss, Papler, and of course Erdmann & Rossi of Berlin.

The new Mercedes-Benz racing cars built to the '750 kg' maximum weight formula were successful on their first appearance. On 3 June the young Prussian aristocrat Manfred von Brauchitsch, now a member of the team, won the *Eifelrennen* at the Nürburg Ring. He nearly did not make it. At the weighing-in the new cars were found to be a couple of pounds too heavy, and it was only by scrubbing their white paintwork down to the bare aluminium that they were brought within the limit. This led some newspapers to call them 'the Silver Arrows.'

In 1932 the A.I.A.C.R. (Alliance Internationale des Automobile-Clubs Reconnus) announced that for the seasons 1934 to 1936 inclusive (later extended to 1937) the maximum weight of cars should not exceed 750 kg (15 cwt) not counting driver, fuel, oil, water, wheels or tyres; that cockpits must measure at least 33½ inches across and that the minimum distance for a Grand Prix should be 500 km (310 miles). A year later, in March 1933, Daimler-Benz let it be known that they would be returning to racing under the new Formula, competitions being an excellent form of publicity. Meanwhile the National Socialist Party, which had just come to power in Germany, also realised the value of motor racing from the propaganda point of view, and allotted substantial subsidies to Daimler-Benz – and to their rivals Auto Union – by way of encouragement. This too may have influenced the Directors' decision. Designed by Dr Hans Nibel and built inside the year by teams led by Wagner (chassis), Heess (engines) and Schilling (super-

chargers) a prototype single-seater was ready in February 1934. Early cars (right) had no headrest, a long tail and an outside handbrake. After preliminary tests at Monza, W 25 reached its definitive shape (below). Principal dimensions were: wheelbase 8 ft 10 in, track (front) 4 ft 9½ in, track (rear) 4 ft 6½ in. The 1934 season, which opened for W 25 with the *Eifelrennen* in which Mercedes met Auto Unions for the first time, brought Daimler-Benz four victories: Manfred von Brauchitsch in the *Eifelrennen,* Luigi Fagioli in the Coppa Acerbo at Leghorn, Caracciola in the Italian Grand Prix and Fagioli again in the Grand Prix of Spain. Fagioli also came second in the German Grand Prix and the G.P. of Czechoslovakia, while in the French Grand Prix at Montlhéry and the Swiss Grand Prix on the Bremgarten circuit all the Mercedes retired. In 1935 the Mercedes-Benz team, comprising Caracciola, von Brauchitsch, Fagioli and Hermann Lang, did even better, winning eight of the ten races in which they took part.

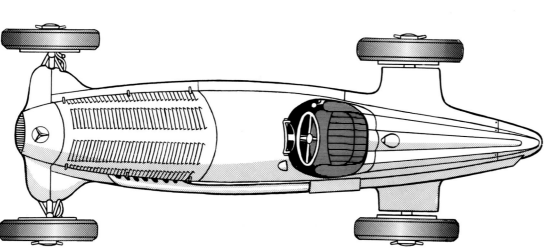

At the rear of the W 25 chassis (below, right) was the four-speed all-indirect gearbox and differential assembly, carried on large diameter tubular cross members. The swinging half-axles comprised tubes containing the drive-shafts, and were sprung by transverse quarter-elliptic leaf springs. Movement of springs and shock-absorbers was limited by the bump-stop seen here, its bracket bolted to the boxed chassis side member.

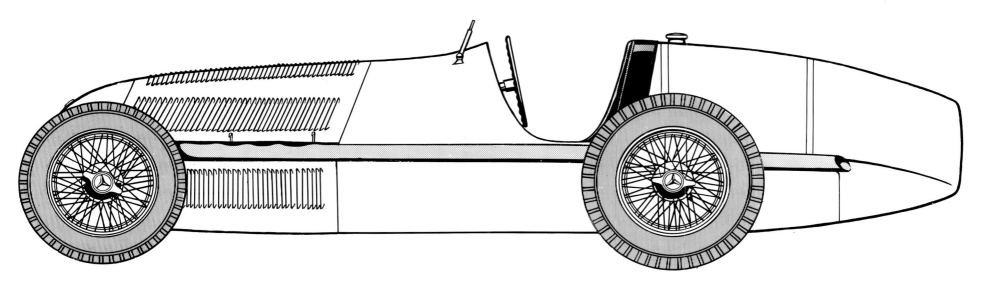

Power for W 25 came from this straight eight with twin overhead camshafts and one plug per cylinder, supercharged by a Roots blower permanently engaged and driven at twice engine speed, supplying two pressurised carburetters. This engine was designed by Albert Heess, who had been responsible for the 1914 Grand Prix engine; his hand is very evident in the separate cylinders and welded steel water-jackets. The capacity and power of this eight-cylinder underwent successive increases: from 3360 cc (78 × 88) and 354 bhp in M 25 A these rose to 3710 cc (82 × 88) and 398 bhp in M 25 AB, 3990 cc (82 × 94.5) and 430 bhp in the M 25 B, and finally 4310 cc (82 × 102) and 462 bhp on the M 25 C.

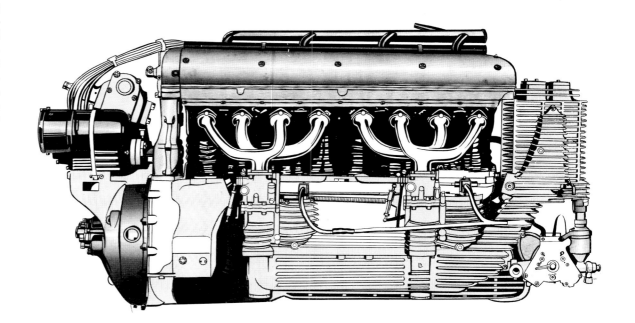

Independent front suspension on W 25 was provided by equal-length wishbones which acted through bell-cranks upon horizontal coil springs inside the tubular front cross member. An extension of the lower wishbone was connected to a friction shock-absorber.

In its original form the W 25 had a long-tailed body without headrest, and the handbrake, Vintage fashion, outside. The car was assigned to von Brauchitsch for preliminary testing, which took place in February 1934 at Monza, followed by further testing at Monza in March, and on the Milan-Varese *autostrada,* when a curved scuttle was used instead of the aero screen.

Two months later bodywork had been finalised and the cars went to Berlin for intensive testing during practice for the *Avusrennen.* They were tried by Caracciola, Brauchitsch and a very experienced newcomer to the team, Luigi Fagioli. But by the morning of race-day they were still not ready, and were withdrawn.

Family likeness. This car is not a non-standard W 25; it is the special streamlined SSKL which Otto Merz drove overnight from Stuttgart to Berlin, only to crash fatally in the morning in practice for the 1933 *Avusrennen*.

The Klausen Pass hill-climb was held for the last time in 1934, when Rudolf Caracciola in this W 25 established an all-time record of 15m 22.20s, winning the Racing class.

Germany showed little interest in record-breaking, traditionally a domain of the French, British and Americans, until 1934, when successful attempts were made by Auto Union. Daimler-Benz were now forced to participate. That autumn, the Racing Department were charged to produce two W 25 cars with 430 bhp M 25 B engine, one with normal bodywork, the other a streamliner with enclosed cockpit (above), unlouvred bonnet and special narrow radiator. No front-wheel brakes were fitted. The two cars were transported to Gyon, near Budapest in October 1934. The open car broke down with supercharger trouble, but in the *Rennlimousine,* Caracciola set a new International Class C (3,000-5000 cc) record for the flying kilometre at an average of 197 mph.

1936 was a disastrous season for Mercedes. To brighten their image they again became involved in pure speed, and with a view to International Class B (5,000-8000 cc) records built the impressive machine shown below. Very sleek with 'spats' enclosing the wheels it used a special V-12 M DAB engine of 5777 cc with two blowers, developing 616 bhp at 5800 rpm in a 1936 Grand Prix chassis. The aerodynamic body was the result of wind-tunnel tests at the Zeppelin works at Friedrichshafen. The car without fuel weighed 1023 kg or roughly $20\frac{1}{2}$ cwt. October 1936, using the Frankfurt-Darmstadt Autobahn alongside Frankfurt aerodrome Caracciola set the following records: 223 mph for the flying kilometre, 228 for the flying mile; plus 5 km at 210, 10 km at 204 mph and 10 miles at 295 mph.

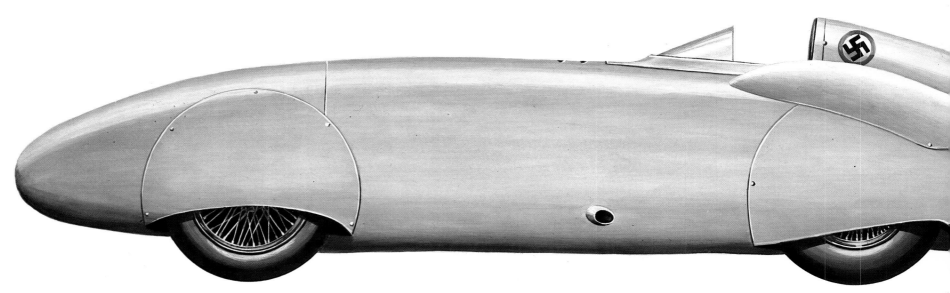

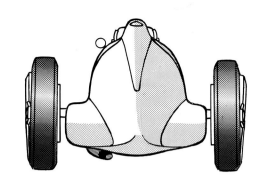

The career of the ME 25 was as short as it was disappointing; this intended replacement for W 25 won only two races in 1936 (Monaco and Tunis), and its poor showing led Mercedes-Benz to withdraw from the last two events of the season. The 1936 ME 25 retained few features of W 25 although derived from it. With capacity increased to 4740 cc (86 × 102) the straight-eight was based on M 25 C and developed 453 bhp at 5800 rpm thanks to improved breathing and a more powerful supercharger. Lighter and shortened to 8 ft wheelbase, the chassis was also modified as to rear suspension, including unsuccessful experiments with De Dion axle. The body was lower, with an almost oval grille, flanked by air-intakes.

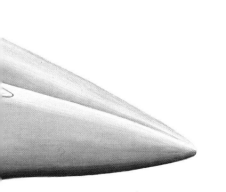
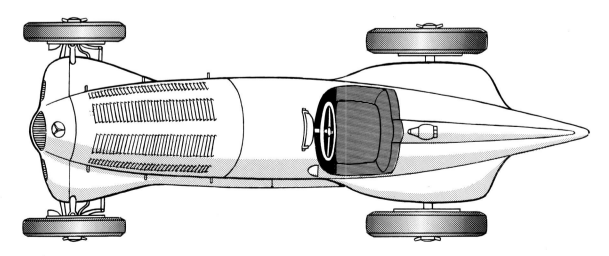

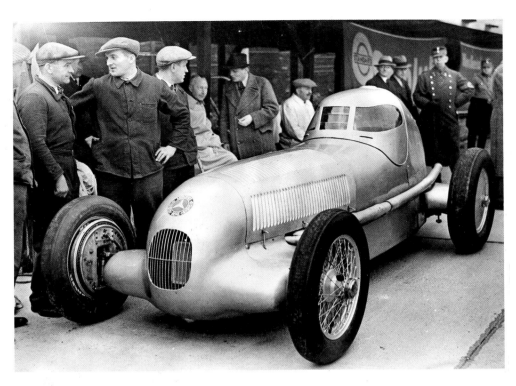

They called this enclosed W 25 the *Rennlimousine*. After setting records at almost 200 mph on the road at Gyon, near Budapest in October 1934, it was given front brakes, 'spats' for the rear wheels, bonnet louvres and a lower 'hard top' in time for the 1935 *Avusrennen*. These three photographs were taken some months before that race, in the course of development sessions. Caracciola is conferring with Alfred Neubauer.

26 October 1936. On a stretch of the Frankfurt-Darmstadt Autobahn alongside Frankfurt aerodrome Caracciola has just broken International Class B records for the flying mile and kilometre at 225 mph, driving a special record car using a non-Formula DAB V-12 engine. Note how air-pressure has stove in the front panelling.

If the 36/220 was first and foremost a competition car, this was rather less true of the new 38/250 or SS type: the latter's waistline was higher and the interior more roomy. The factory no longer sold only open bodywork, but supplied saloons and coupés.

Two versions of the SS were designed purely for racing: the 27/170/225 with 6.2:1 compression ratio and the 27/180/250. Both these engines, running on petrol/benzole mixtures, were raced by the factory until 1931.

Hardly had the SS appeared than Mercedes-Benz announced a new variant: the SSK or Model 720, the K as usual standing for *kurz*. The SSK was indeed short, having a wheelbase of less than 10 ft, for this model was originally designed for speed hillclimbs. The SSK made its debut at the Gabelbach event on 29 July 1928 in the hands of Rudolf Caracciola, where it established a new record at 109.3 kph. Three weeks later it won the Freiburg-Schauinsland climb at 73 kph, and not long afterwards won also at Semmering, where Caracciola established yet another new record. The model was still winning prizes in 1935.

In racing trim the SSK was known at the factory as WS06, where men in the tuning department like Albert Heess succeeded in raising the power to 300 bhp thanks to an oversize supercharger (the famous 'Elephant' blower) and a c.r. of 6:1. On some hill-climb assignments the blower was never disengaged at all, and for this reason these cars — and there said to be only two made — were called 27/300, with no mention of peak power unblown.

Even today the SSK must be regarded as one of the most beautiful and sophisticated of all racing cars — making due allowance for technical progress, of course. It may be compared with the big $6^{1}/_{2}$-litre Bentleys which Ettore Bugatti called the fastest lorries in the world. The combat between these models at Le Mans in 1930 was one of the most exciting episodes in the history of motor racing; and although victory at Le Mans eventually went to the Bentleys, there were

very few occasions indeed when the SSK had to acknowledge defeat. In fact, Caracciola's lone 38/260 at Le Mans was pitted against *two* full teams of Bentleys — the Speed Sixes from the Works and H.R.S. Birkin's blower $4^{1}/_{2}$s. Caracciola utterly defeated the Blower team, which broke its engines and destroyed its tyres in trying to keep up. He eventually retired during the night, a defective dynamo being blamed. Normally, the Mercedes made best performance in its class, and the six-cylinder engine was renowned for long life and reliability. Attention was given to cooling on the SSK, the sump, blower, induction manifold, shock-absorbers and brake-drums all being finned.

At $31^{3}/_{4}$ cwt (1570 kilos) the SSK chassis was 260 lb (120 kilos) lighter than that of the SS, while the stark two-seater body weighed only 440 lb (200 kilos).

Caracciola was allowed by Alfred Neubauer to choose the events in which he wished to compete. In 1929 he entered for the Monaco Grand Prix, a 'round-the-houses' race through the streets of Monte Carlo which was *formule libre*, i.e., open to all comers. Caracciola and his SSK finished third. No doubt a larger fuel tank would have enabled him to win, for pitstops for refuelling cost him precious seconds. He failed to win the German Grand Prix, retiring with a broken con-rod while in the lead, but in 1930 he won the (sports car) Irish Grand Prix in Phoenix Park, Dublin, and broke the record for the Semmering Pass hill-climb. He won the German hill-climb championship (sports cars) in both 1930 and 1931.

In 1931 Caracciola was forced to compete privately once more. Daimler-Benz, like many other manufacturers, could no longer afford the expense of maintaining a works team in the depths of the Depression which followed the Wall Street crash of 1929. This withdrawal, however, did not mean the abandonment, or even the suspension of the company's efforts on behalf of motoring competition, for cars as an instrument of sport continued to exert an irresistible fascination on their customers, and every success was

At Monaco in 1937 a bitter duel developed ▷ between von Brauchitsch (10) and Caracciola (8), to Alfred Neubauer's despair but the delight of spectators. They are seen here at the Station hairpin. All ended well, however, with Brauchitsch and Caracciola first and second, Kautz third and Zehender fifth in similar cars.

A Mercedes-Benz lying second? This picture from the 1936 *Eifelrennen,* of Fagioli tailing Raymond Sommer's Alfa Romeo, symbolises that disastrous season when Mercedes were dogged by mechanical and road-holding problems.

This picture (above left) shows Caracciola during the Donington Grand Prix, final event of the 1937 season. He finished third behind Manfred von Brauchitsch (above right) who, after leading the race at half-distance was overtaken by Bernd Rosemeyer's Auto Union. These photographs show the sheer size of the '750 kg' Formula cars.

Swiss Grand Prix 1937. Caracciola took the lead comfortably during the opening laps of the Bremgarten circuit, Berne – his favourite, with the Nürburg Ring – and no-one could dislodge him. The other W 125s (Hermann Lang, Manfred von Brauchitsch and the Swiss driver Christian Kautz) came second, third and sixth.

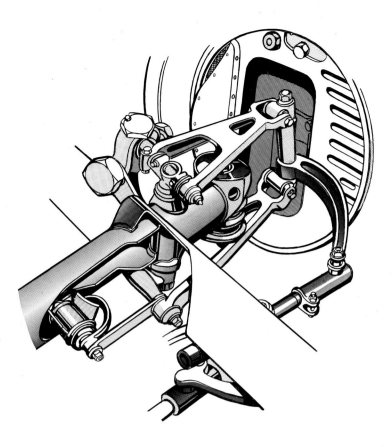

A new Formula governing Grand Prix racing was to have come into force in 1937; but between the initial discussions and its final adoption seven months elapsed, and it was decided to extend the 1934-1936 '750 kg' Formula for another year. Research undertaken by Daimler-Benz with a view to building a car to comply with the Regulations proposed but not adopted (3460 cc maximum, 850 kg minimum weight) resulted in W 125 – a transitional between WE 25 of 1936 and W 154 of 1938. For 1937 Albert Heess completely redesigned the engine, for although the stroke remained unaltered the bore was enlarged to 94 mm, giving a swept volume of 5660 cc, and a new crankshaft with nine main bearings instead of five resulted in an engine that was both stronger and longer than before. Yet Heess managed to insert it in W 125 chassis which had been designed for a 3½-litre! Fundamental changes were made to supercharging arrangements. After the 1932 *Eifelrennen* Daimler-Benz at last abandoned their cherished plan of blowing pure air, and arranged for the supercharger to draw mixture from the carburetters. This engine gave more than 600 bhp. Driven by Caracciola, Brauchitsch and Lang W 125 won seven out of eleven races. Rear suspension was by De Dion axle and torsion bars.

Front springing on W 125 resembled that of production 500 and 540 K models (cf page 52). The wishbone assembly allowed a small amount of radial float, being mounted on a vertical pivot passing through the front cross tube of the chassis. Movement was limited by a 'kick shackle' on the frame (lower left in the drawing) linked to the lower wishbone. Note also the hydraulic damper and the linking shaft between steering-arm and track-rod made necessary by the floating wishbone.

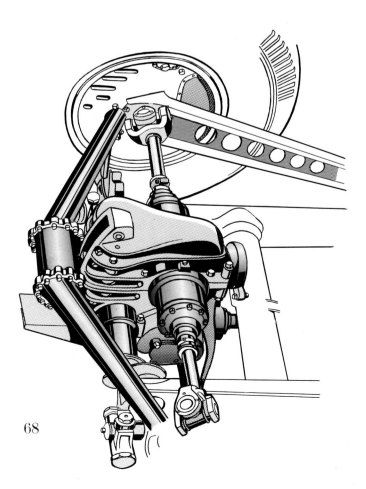

Rear suspension on W 125 (opposite, left) comprised a De Dion tube carrying the wheels, the short centre portion containing an articulated joint. The tube was located sideways by a hardened steel ball forming part of the centre section, which moved up and down in a slot at the back of the gearbox/differential casing. This drawing shows also the pot-type inboard universals on the drive shafts, and the girderlike radius-cum-torque arms, which were attached at the front by ball joints to the chassis. Springing was by longitudinal torsion-bars, the anchorages of which were situated above the front and rear ends of the torque arms. Hydraulic dampers were mounted on the rear cross-tube, arms parallel with the drive shafts.

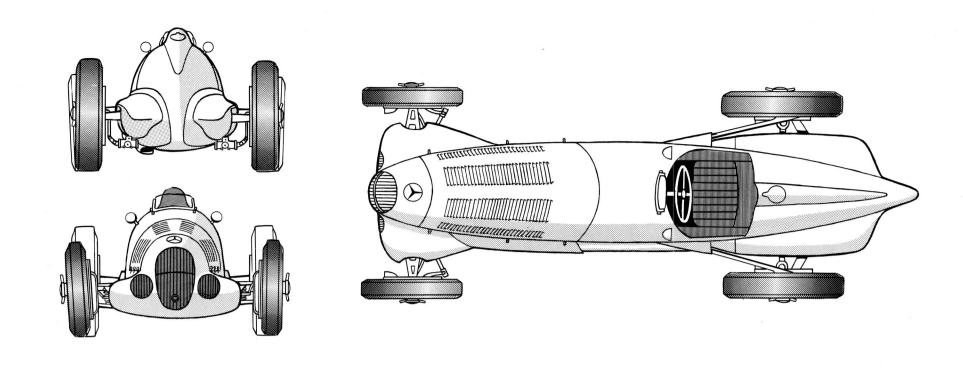

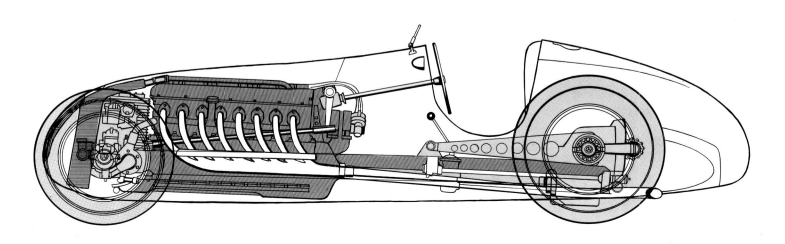

69

In the Mercedes-Benz pits the work of the three mechanics allotted to each of the cars was carried out with exemplary precision. Stops to refuel and change all four wheels took no more than 28 to 35 seconds, and fuel was put in through pressure hoses at the rate of 5 gallons a second. The cars are those of Lang and Caracciola, 1937.

Dick Seaman, who tried to offset the swastika on the tail of his car by wearing a British-racing-green linen helmet, was engaged by Mercedes-Benz at the start of the 1937 season. His second race for them was the Vanderbilt Cup, on the twisty Roosevelt Raceway, Long Island, N.Y., and if he had not run short of petrol three laps from the end he might well have won. As it was he came second to Bernd Rosemeyer's Auto Union.

For the 1937 Coppa Acerbo at Pescara on the baking Adriatic coast, the front of von Brauchitsch's W 125 was given four extra air inlets. Victory went to Auto Union, but Mercedes-Benz came second.

reflected in the balance sheet. This being so the company were glad to assist their talented ex-driver by offering him the latest SSK on very advantageous terms, properly tuned and prepared, and with the services of the Works racing mechanics, Wilhelm Sebastian and Willy Zimmer. Development engineers brought in from the Benz works at Mannheim now that Porsche had gone, included Hans Nibel (of Benz *Tropfenwagen* fame), Max Wenger and Fritz Nallinger, all of whom did their best to make Caracciola's SSK even faster and more reliable.

Their efforts culminated during the spring of 1931 in the production of a special 720 SSK in a chassis lightened wherever weight could be saved. In the early twenties, when he designed the central-engined *Tropfenwagen* Grand Prix car built by Benz in 1924, Hans Nibel had used a chassis pierced with large circular orifices, these being the best means of economising weight without unduly reducing rigidity. At the same time the clutch and brake pedals, hand-brake, back-plates and all brackets etc., wherever possible were drilled for lightness. Thanks to this slimming-cure Caracciola's car lost 125 kilos. Italian, French and British manufacturer were no strangers to the drilling of pedals and brackets, but no-one had dared to perforate the chassis frame itself. On the special Mercedes the only parts spared were the main side-members forward of the bulkhead. To the name of this SSK therefore was added another letter: L for *Leicht.* Here then was the SSKL, lightest of the breed.

Rudolf Caracciola's first season with the SSKL began brilliantly with victory in the 1931 Mille Miglia, 1000 miles of racing on public roads, and the only occasion when a German driver won that event at the wheel of a German car. Immediately afterwards he won the *Avusrennen* on the Avus track at Berlin, the *Eifelrennen* at the Nürburg Ring and the German Grand Prix, also held at the Ring. This was the first occasion when the Mercedes long-handled racing jack

was used, an invention of W. Sebastian and Willy Walb. Caracciola and his SSK became inseparable.

Officially only seven SSKL were made. Later several of the thirty-one SSK cars previously built were lightened and promoted to the rank of SSKL although lacking some of the special 'mods', including the 'Elephant' blower which provided much of the power. When one of these quasi-SSKLs comes to light nowadays it should be regarded with indulgence, and not dismissed out of hand. It may be that the work of lightening was carried out during the working life of the car, nearly forty years ago, and should therefore be entitled to respect. On the other hand certain ostensible SSKL cars that have come upon the market in recent years have turned out to be no more than replicas, even though certain of the parts may be original. Around the 1960s there were people in the Middle West of America who specialised in producing cars of this kind, for it was fashionable to boast of having 'discovered' in some old barn or shed a supercharged Mercedes, preferably a 'genuine SSKL'.

As the 1931 season drew to its close, Works backing entirely dried up. Neubauer could obtain not a Mark more for his protégé, and Caracciola went into partnership with his friend Louis Chiron to drive *monoposto* Alfa Romeos. In his place two *independants*, Hans Stuck and Manfred von Brauchitsch, took up the torch for Mercedes, both men having sufficient means to support an SSKL in the style to which it was accustomed without financial assistance from Untertürckheim. Manfred von Brauchitsch's SSKL was actually lighter than standard. Stuck shipped his to South America for a season of *formule libre* racing in Brazil and Argentina. His most noted achievement was winning the Rio de Janeiro to Petropolis event, over a distance of 60 kilometres. He was still there when entries closed for the 1932 *Avusrennen,* and so Brauchitsch became favourite with the German crowds.

The Avus track (today, alas, cut in half by the Berlin

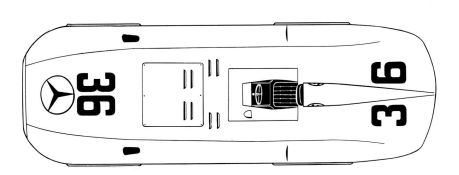

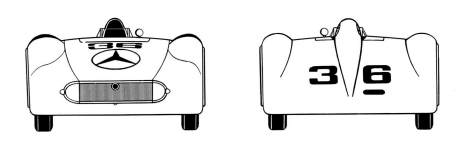

The steeply banked Avus track at Berlin was easily the fastest circuit in the world. In 1937 the 122-mile *formule libre* race called the *Avusrennen* served as a test-bed for three composite streamliners. Hermann Lang's car (above) comprised a 1936 chassis, extended at both ends and fitted with an M 125 straight eight of 5.7 litres. The new body was lower than that of the 1936 record-breaker, and wide enough to enclose the wheels. It had a rectangular grille and air outlets in the flanks. On race day it was decided not to use the hinged wheel-panels tried one month previously: they made the tyres overheat, and had little effect on streamlining. With its special track-racing ratios Lang's car at 5500 rpm was doing 95 mph in lst, 150 mph in 2nd, 180 mph in 3rd and almost 230 mph in top. His winning speed was 162.61 mph, with a best lap at 167 mph. The W 125 of Manfred von Brauchitsch (left) was identical as to bodywork (except for a air slots above the front wings) but equipped with 5.6-litre (82 × 88) V-12 M DAB engine built for record-breaking.

Under the aegis of the *Oberste Nationale Sportbehörde für die Deutsche Kraftfahrt* – the Supreme Authority for German Motoring Sport – Mercedes-Benz and Auto Union were bidden to participate in a special Record Week on the Frankfurt-Darmstadt motorway in October 1937. Daimler-Benz built a special streamlined car for the occasion similar to the Avus V-12, but with 'sprint' engine developing 679 bhp at 5800 rpm for theoretical maxima of 230 mph at 5500 and 260 at 6000 rpm. Caracciola however could not improve on Bernd Rosemeyer's best, 248 mph in the Auto Union.

For the 1937 *Avusrennen,* a *formule libre* event on the now steeply banked and tremendously fast Avus circuit at Berlin Daimler-Benz entered a variegated team: Caracciola (35) drove a lengthened and streamlined W 125, von Brauchitsch (36) a streamlined W 125 with DAB V-12 engine developed for record-breaking. Lang's car, (37) was a 1936 G.P. machine lengthened, streamlined and fitted with M 125 engine; Dick Seaman had a standard W 125. The race was in three heats, and Lang was the winner, at 163 mph.

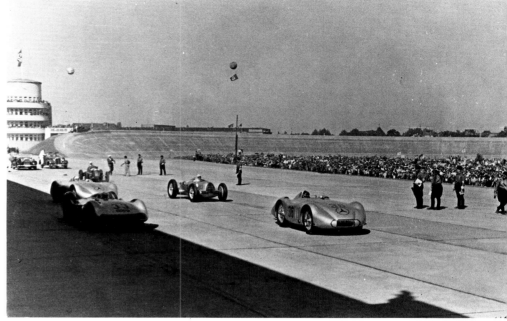

The 1938 Mercedes-Benz record car was even cleaner aerodynamically than its predecessors. Cooling was by means of an ice tank, so that the two air inlets served only the special Type DAB 5.66-litre V-12 engine. The running-gear was W 125. On 28 January 1938, on the Frankfurt-Darmstadt motorway Caracciola covered a flying kilometre at 268 mph, easily the highest speed ever reached on the road. Later that day while attempting to beat this record in a streamlined Auto Union Bernd Rosemeyer was killed.

After a year during which the extended '750 kg' Formula continued to apply, new A.I.A.C.R. Regulations were announced in September 1936, to come into force for 1938. These imposed a minimum weight ranging from 400 kg to 850 kg according to the size and type of engine; the latter might vary in capacity from 1000 cc to 4500 cc if unsupercharged, and from 666 cc to 3000 cc if supercharged. In practice this meant $4\frac{1}{2}$ and 3 litres respectively. By March 1937 Daimler-Benz had new Grand Prix cars on the stocks. The Racing Department naturally, in view of their vast experience with blowers, took the 3-litre option, and mindful of the DAB 5.6 litre's success the previous year, settled for a V-12. In the spring of 1938 W 154 was ready for testing at Monza. By the end of that season, having been raced in eight international events by Caracciola, von Brauchitsch, Lang and the English driver R.J.B. Seaman, Mercedes had won five times (French Grand Prix, German G.P., Coppa Ciano, Coppa Acerbo, Swiss Grand Prix), with five second places and four thirds.

The 1938 3-litre W 154 chassis, based closely on W 125, comprised two oval-tube longerons and four tubular cross members, rigidity of the rear portion being reinforced by four pierced longitudinal stringers. At the front was the 2962 cc V-12, inclined backwards and offset at angle of 6 degrees; at the back, a five-speed gearbox in unit with the differential. The De Dion axle, articulated as before, was located laterally by a ball-joint moving vertically in a slot behind the diff. casing. Note the torsion bars, parallel with the frame, and the torque arms located at the central cross tube.

74

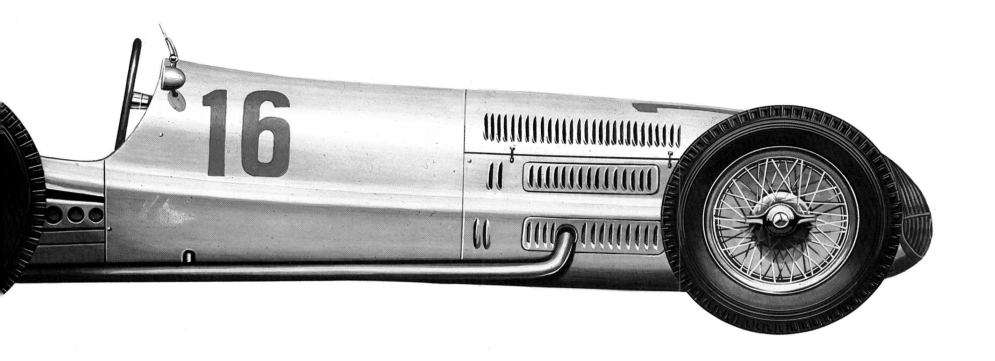

By inclining the short-stroke V-12 engine and passing the prop-shaft to one side of the driver's seat Daimler-Benz engineers succeeded in building a remarkably low car: the body (not counting the headrest) came no higher than the back tyres. The wheelbase, at 8 ft 11$\frac{1}{2}$ in was nearly three inches shorter than W 125. Consuming special methanol 'dope' at the rate of 3 mpg, the car required not only a 48-gallon tank in the tail but a 40-gallon saddle tank under the scuttle. A common filler was used, with balance pipes beside the driver's seat. Some 433 to 474 bhp were developed, depending on type of carburetter, to propel an all-up starting line weight of 24.1 cwt at 170 mph.

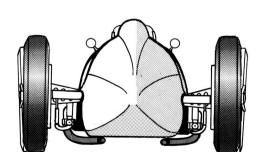

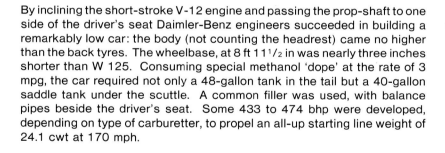

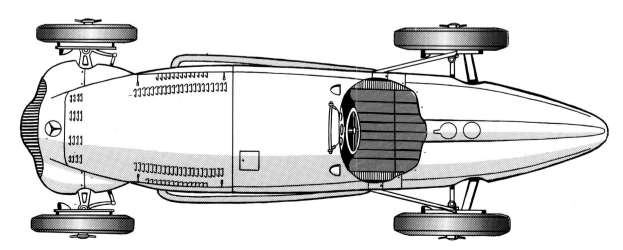

Wall) being built for high speeds, Brauchitsch briefed a famous aerodynamicist, Baron Reinhard von Koenig-Fachsenfeld, to design him a streamlined body. Built by Vetter of Bad Cannstatt and nicknamed 'the Zeppelin on wheels', this car proved slower than expected when originally tried, and road-holding was not very good. But in the race itself Brauchitsch excelled himself, winning at 120 mph (194 kph), a clear 6 kph faster than Rudolf Caracciola's Alfa.

Neubauer meanwhile had never stopped lobbying his Directors. In 1933 he managed to push through a special streamlined body for the SSKL – although no-one at Untertürckheim could see the SSKL as a serious rival to the lightweights from Bugatti, Maserati and Alfa Romeo. But *formule libre* (which set no limits on engine-capacity or weight, governing only the length or duration of races) still had a year to run, and permission was given for the car to be raced. Neubauer had hoped with this special SSKL to tempt Caracciola back into the team; but this plan came to nought. Driving his white-and-blue Scuderia CC (Caracciola/Chiron) Alfa Romeo, Rudi crashed in practice for the 1933 Monaco Grand Prix, seriously breaking his thigh. Neubauer had to look elsewhere to find another pilot for his new streamlined monster.

His choice fell on the stalwart Otto Merz who, always game for a lark, accepted immediately, not caring even when told that the car would not be ready until a few hours before practice opened. In fact it was later than that; there was no time for lorries or transporters; Merz had to take it himself. Without wasting a moment he leapt into this completely strange car and drove through the night from Stuttgart to Berlin – non-stop and without headlights, for the car was not road-equipped. Luckily he had a full moon and clear skies. Merz and the SSKL made the Avus safe and sound. But now the weather changed. It came on to rain in torrents.

Manfred von Brauchitsch was there with his own streamlined Mercedes which had gone so well the previous year, and a tremendous duel was expected between these two giants. But alas, poor Otto Merz, exhausted by his all-night drive and unable to control his car on the slippery wet Avus *pavé*, failed to complete even one lap of practice. The SSKL left the track and he was killed instantaneously.

Next day, luck deserted Brauchitsch as well. Five times tyre trouble brought him in to the pits, and victory went to Achille Varzi in a 4.9-litre Bugatti, with Count Czaikowski second in another 'four-nine' and Tazio Nuvolari third. And so, for once, Mercedes-Benz finished a season without glory.

The end of the SSK's reign did not mean, of course, an end to supercharger research. Mercedes were much identified now with supercharged cars, and this was the moment to cash in, equating supercharged engines with prestige. Thus the *Grosser Mercedes* – and Big Mercedes it was, with its vast bodywork and 7.7 litres of engine – could be had with a supercharger. This 770 model (W 07 to the Works) was listed from 1930 until 1939 as a 30/150/200, its straight-eight 7655 cc engine having a bore and stroke of 96×135 mm and producing 145 bhp unblown or 200 blown. The supercharger here was not to delight the enthusiast, but simply to make the car go. Gone was the overhead camshaft of glorious memory. This big pushrod ohv engine was designed for quietness and flexibility rather than power and the huge car would hardly do 65 mph. A blower was almost essential.

The 770 was designed as a state carriage for senior officials and captains of industry, but more modest models were available too. The 380 supercharged model which came out in 1933 is a good example. Known at the works as W 22 but often referred to unofficially as the 15/90/120, the 380 was a push-rod straight eight (78×100) of 3820 cc designed for long life. The 380 was the first production Mercedes to have a four-speed gearbox with direct drive on third. Fourth was geared up for effortless cruising on the new Continental motorways, having a ratio of 0.76:1.

The new V-12 developed for the 3-litre Formula which replaced the '750 kg' regulations in 1938 had a Roots blower for each bank, and produced 400 bhp. The Mercedes-Benz team comprising (from left to right) von Brauchitsch, Seaman, Lang and Caracciola, went from strength to strength, winning five out of eight major races, with five second places and four thirds.

Built specially for hill-climbs, this short-chassis W 154 used twin rear wheels; note too the slim radiator cowl made possible by glycol cooling. Hermann Lang here makes best time of the day at Vienna in June 1939.

For the 1938 Grand Prix at Donington von Brauchitsch's car had auxiliary fuel tanks in the scuttle, the filler cap for which may be seen behind the bonnet. He is here seen leading Seaman and Lang. For the third time that season victory eluded Mercedes-Benz. The race went to Nuvolari's Auto Union, with Lang second, Seaman third and von Brauchitsch fifth.

Although similar to the 1938 M 154 the 1939 engine had been sufficiently modified to receive a new Type number: 163. General specification was unchanged: 2962 cc (67 × 70) V-12 with 4 valves and 1 sparking-plug per cylinder and 4 o.h.c., dry-sump lubrication, cooling by 100 per cent glycol and 2 Roots blowers gear-driven from the crank. But now instead of two equal-sized blowers in parallel the engine had two-stage supercharging, developed by Dr Porsche under the code name R 108, by two compressors of unequal size mounted in series. It differed from M 154 in having: wider crankcase, two-stage supercharging, easier maintenance, greater robustness (and weight, 273 kg instead of 252), a lower rev-limit but more power (480 bhp at 7800 rpm).

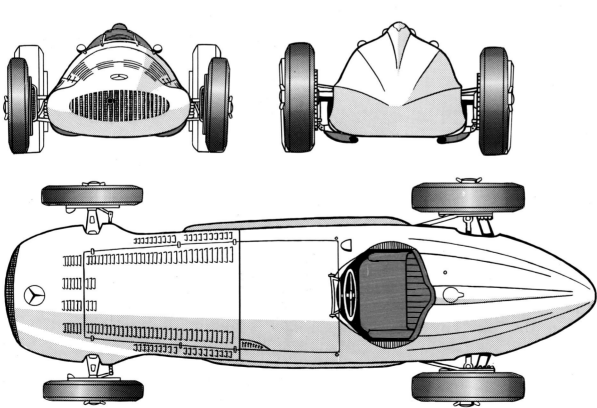

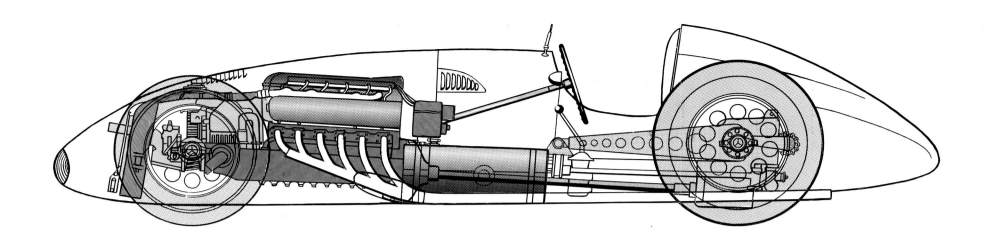

The cars raced in 1939 – and sometimes erroneously called W 163 – all had W 154 chassis and new bodywork; the engine could be M 154, M 154 with R 108 two-stage supercharging, or M 163. The new bodies gave more protection to the driver, being higher in the flank; rear suspension elements were almost enclosed, radiator cowls lower. The brakes now had turbo cooling fins and the drums were pierced with ten holes. The cut-away drawing (above) shows some of the features of W 154/M 163, notably (from left to right): the small radiator for cooling the fuel (to prevent vapour lock); the carburetter air-intake; the glycol radiator; the carburetter; one of the superchargers; the V-12 engine sloping towards the rear; the oil tank; the girder-like torque-arm, below which can be seen the near-side torsion bar; the propeller-shaft; the gearbox/differential assembly; the De Dion axle; a hydraulic shock-absorber. The rear fuel tank, smaller than that of the 1938 W 154 held 50 gallons and a central tank, between bulkhead and dash, 41 gallons. A single filler orifice faired into the headrest, served both tanks. If the 1938 3-litre Mercedes had done well, winning five out of the eight races in which they started, the 1939 cars did even better, being beaten on only two occasions: at the French G.P., when all retired, and in the Grand Prix of Jugoslavia in which they took second place. They won the Pau Grand Prix, *Eifelrennen,* Belgian Grand Prix – marred by the fatal accident to Richard Seaman – German G.P. and G.P. of Switzerland before the outbreak of war brought motoring sport to an end.

Second was 1.83:1 and first 2.86:1. The 10 ft 6 in (3200 mm) wheelbase 380 was sold in short-chassis form, 10 ft 3¹/₂ in (3140 mm), as the 380 K. Both models were supercharged, and of the 151 cars built a few had the blower in unit with the crankcase and produced slightly more power. A few 380s were unsupercharged. The only difference between the 380 engine and the 380 K lay in the maximum revs – 3600 rpm on the 380 K and 3400 on the 380. Contrariwise, the 380 K weighed 2 cwt (100 kilos) more than the 380.

The 380/380K of 1933-34 was a modern motor car, quite easy to drive and with independent suspension all round. At the front there were coil springs and wishbones; the back had coil springs and the famous Mercedes swinging half-axles. The very rigid frame made possible by this form of construction was exceptional on cars of this size, for all-round independent suspension had only been seen on very much smaller cars – including the 170 and 200 Mercedes-Benz. When the big heavy 380 series appeared in 1933 at the Berlin motor show, it aroused much comment amongst competitors and in the motoring Press. Today we are accustomed to cars that are more comfortable and refined in many ways, but in its day the Mercedes swing axle system marked a considerable advance over the old rigid rear axle beam. The magazine *Motor und Sport* remarked that it took courage and self-confidence to attack problems from an unorthodox standpoint, in the design of any car, touring or racing; but that those qualities had 'always been the apanage of the Untertürckheim works'. They regarded the 380 as a link between 'the very latest trends in automobile engineering and the *nec plus ultra* of the classic school, represented by the 36/220 SS'.

The 380 was described as a sports car although it was actually a saloon. However, to have produced a true sports/racing car – on the lines of the SSK – given the economic situation in Germany at that time would have been financially and commercially mad. Grand

Prix cars like the Type 35 Bugatti and SSK Mercedes for sale to wealthy enthusiasts were a thing of the past, although Maserati and Alfa Romeo still made G.P. cars for sale to private entrants like Trossi, Etancelin, Earl Howe, Whitney Straight, Bira, Fontes and the rest, and E.R.A. and Maserati made 1500 cc voiturettes to sell in England, France, Italy and Switzerland, and 1100 cc racers could be had off the peg from M.G. and Maserati; 750 cc M.G. Midgets too. Grand Prix racing had become an affair for specialised vehicles. Meanwhile those who enjoyed driving 'ordinary' cars in competition found no shortage of popular models. While the German Government preached 'motoring for the masses', the sport could not remain a privilege for the few, and a 2000 km Round-Germany Rally was held to whip up popular enthusiasm.

There was always a demand, too, for big high-powered *grand tourisme* cars for use on Europe's growing motorway network, while the 'wishful thinkers' of the time were for ever predicting recovery, which encouraged manufacturers great and small to find money for investment.

The Mercedes-Benz range at this time included a 170, the 370 'Mannheim' (a large dull side-valve survivor from Benz), 200, 290; the *Grosser Mercedes* headed this list alongside the supercharged 380. A well-known motoring writer, Stefan von Szenasy, said that sports cars were evolving closer and closer to touring cars 'of which the 380 was an especially rapid example'; he had already described the SS 38/250 as a sports or racing machine on touring-car lines. He pointed out that the 380 was thoroughly practical to use and maintain, and had only been called a sports car because of its high power and excellent handling. Its output of 32 bhp per litre and 63 bhp per ton were considered excellent at the time.

The 380 was available as a four-door saloon and with 'Cabriolet' (all-weather) bodies designated A, B, C and D. Cabriolet A was what the British called an

Rudi Caracciola goes it alone. After the retirement of Lang and von Brauchitsch Caracciola's was the only Mercedes left in the 1939 German Grand Prix. He drove a brilliantly planned race, thus adding a final victory to his long career with Mercedes-Benz.

The last event of the 1939 season (and of the 3-litre Formula) was held through the cobbled, tram-lined streets of Belgrade on 3 September, the day Great Britain and France declared war on Germany following the invasion of Poland. Only two W 154 Mercedes, two Auto Unions and a Bugatti took part. Manfred von Brauchitsch (6) took the lead at first; a few laps later Hermann Lang was struck by a stone flug up by his team-mate's car and retired. Brauchitsch eventually spun, and victory went to Tazio Nuvolari's Auto Union.

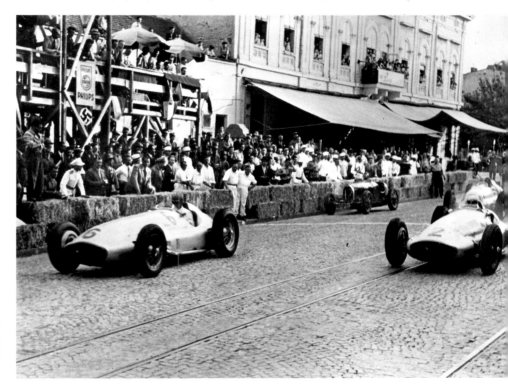

81

Two cars in one

'occasional four-seater drophead' with two doors, two proper seats and cramped accommodation behind. Suitcases could be supplied to fit the reasonably roomy trunk on the back. Cabriolet B was a proper four-seater 'four-light' drophead, for although there were only two doors it had an extra small window ('quarter-light') each side; the bonnet was not quite so long as that of Cabriolet A. Cabriolet C was also a four-seater convertible but without glass in the quarters. The Cabriolet D convertible had four doors and would seat five persons. Also listed were a two-seater roadster with light disappearing hood and an open tourer with detachable sidescreens.

According to tests carried out at the factory on 21 March 1933 a Cabriolet A on its geared-up fourth speed of 0.60:1 attained exactly 160 kph (100 mph). An identical car with 0.64 overdrive fourth did 139 kph and neither car exceeded 3600 rpm. (Sic. Official works figures.) The overdrive ratio fitted as standard was 0.76, with a 5.11 back axle, although some models had a 0.70 fourth. The 380 K (which, remember, was heavier than the 380) could also be had with lower first (3.41 instead of 2.86) and second (1.8 instead of 1.6) ratios in the gearbox. Third, of course was direct. A few 380s were sold without supercharger.

Mercedes-Benz pursued an extraordinary marketing policy: all 380 saloon and cabriolets cost exactly the same — 19,500 Marks irrespective of style, and the price of a bare chassis was 13,000 Marks. This policy was continued on later models, thus any 500 K cost exactly 22,000 Marks.

In 1934 Daimler-Benz made a batch of 380s in which the engine was bored out to 80 mm; and in fact no two batches were exactly alike, as there were alterations to front and rear track. The road-holding and ride were much praised. The use of a partially boxed underslung chassis brought the centre of gravity down and the all-independent suspension, by coil springs and wishbones in front and coil springs and swing-axles behind, gave a better ride on the roads of the period than many a more expensive car. The car's habit of kicking its heels in the air under braking as weight came off the rear end was not considered objectionable, for people were used to the bumps and jolting of ordinary leaf springs and axles; a 36/220 felt like a mammoth at full gallop compared with the 380. The latter accelerated from 0 to 100 kph in only 22 seconds; the blower came in at 25 mph — reached in 7 seconds — which was not unimpressive.

At the time when the 380 came out finishing touches were being put at Untertürckheim to a larger and more powerful straight eight, coded W 24. This too was a pushrod ohv design, of 86 × 100 bore and stroke, and 5019 cc, which claimed to produce 100 bhp unblown and 160 with supercharger. This engine was announced the following year when it powered the 380 replacement — the Mercedes-Benz 500 K.

The Works test car was shod with exceptionally fat tyres (7.50 × 17), although production models had 6.50 × 17. Most of the 500s were given limousine bodywork on the long chassis (3290 mm, 10 ft 9½ in wheelbase); the two-seater Cabriolet, two-seater roadster and fixed-head coupé were built on a shorter 9 ft 8½ in (2980 mm) chassis and called 500 K.

Journalists wishing to road test the big blown 5-litre found their way anything but clear. Even staff writers on the *Allgemeine Automobil-Zeitung* were refused an opportunity to drive. They had to make do with 'road impressions' from the passenger's seat: 'Even when Herr Merten took narrow and sinuous secondary roads at more than 80 mph not a moment's anxiety was felt...'. Herr Merten brushed compliments aside; the credit was due not to him, he said, but to the car's excellent road-holding. 'Any child could have done just as well' he added — which cannot have gone down well with the Press.

The 500 K, said the *Allgemeine Automobil-Zeitung*, should not be regarded as a sports model but as a 'rapid everyday vehicle whose 80 mph cruising speed could be bettered only by an aeroplane'. The same journal made acceleration tests on overdrive fourth and the direct-drive third, starting from 25 mph, 'the most favourable speed for the engine' – i.e., the minimum speed at which the blower would come in. 'In overdrive the car went from 50 mph to 70 mph (80 kph to 110 kph) in 12.8 seconds; in third it picked up from 60 kph to 100 kph (say 35 to 60 mph) in little more than 7 seconds. Over this speed range, so much used when pulling away from obstructions or slow corners, the acceleration works out at 1.6 m/s^2.'

Herr Merten had no difficulty in slowing his 2^1/$_3$ tons (2350 kilos) of motorcar from high speed. 'Thanks to the hydraulic brakes aided by Bosch vacuum servo, the driver has no need to exert excessive pressure on the pedal' said the writer, who had not been driving. Cars of this kind did require a good deal of force to operate the brakes and clutch, and when one samples any of these big Classics today, whether Mercedes, Horch, Maybach or Isotta-Fraschini – none of them intended for the husky enthusiast – they do demand rather an effort although no-one thought so at the time. The *Allgemeine Automobil-Zeitung* was full of praise for the sweetness of the gear-change and the car's manoeuvrability in town traffic.

Customers praised the quietness and flexibility of the engine. 'Thanks to the supercharger', wrote one to the London offices of Mercedes-Benz, 'the 500 K is really two cars in one. I have a smart and reliable touring car for everyday use, and at the same time a high-performance sports car for which no corner is too sharp, no hill too steep, no situation too delicate'.

Despite the fact that the car with limousine body weighed 2^1/$_2$ tons unladen – the chassis alone weighing 6 cwt (300 kg) more than that of a 380 – the car would do 100 mph (160 kph). A 500 K road-tested by *The Autocar* was clocked at 85 mph after a standing quarter-mile, and the testers concluded that 'Even at 95-100 mph the car remains stable and easy to drive. The engine is quiet and free from vibration. There is much power in reserve, even at low speeds'.

Fears that the supercharger might do more harm than good to the engine in the long term proved groundless. For one thing there was no straight road long enough and empty enough for the car to be held flat out, mile after mile, with the blower engaged; besides, the din from the supercharger, and the fuel consumption, caused drivers to think twice. Even at thirties prices 8 mpg cost a lot. However, it was quite unnecessary to use the blower all the time. Without it there was ample power at half throttle: hills of 1 in 7 or more could be taken in fourth without the blower. Most drivers started in second, and kept first for re-starting on hills. As in the 380, fourth was geared up, for economical cruising. It was not necessary to declutch when changing up or down between third and fourth: one simply released the accelerator, paused in neutral and in it went. In overdrive fourth the car would run smoothly down to 25 mph and even accelerate away without snatch.

If there was a weak point, it was starting. Few people could find the right setting for the mixture control on the steering column. One had also to remember to turn on the auxiliary two-gallon gravity tank which supplied fuel for the first mile or so, because pressure for raising it from the rear-mounted petrol tank took some while to build up. The engine once started, it was necessary to let it warm up for five minutes on the hand throttle before one could drive away. When the car had stood outside in cold weather, too, it was hard to change gear until the oil in the gearbox was warm.

The 500 series was quickly superseded by the 540/540 K, a prototype of which model (coded W 24) covered some thousands of miles in 1934. Production models were not ready until 1936 and these, like their 5-litre predecessors, were known by the Works number W 29. This was because experimental cars of both series had been fitted with a De Dion rear axle, but by the time they were ready for production, policy dictated the use of swing-axles to match the rest of the Mercedes range. The new pushrod straight-eight was

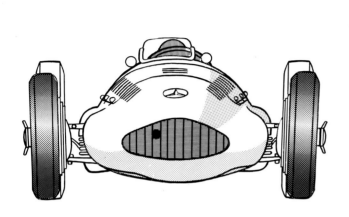

Although the fatal accident to Rosemeyer in January 1938 had blunted the Germans' enthusiasm for record-breaking, Daimler-Benz was ready for a new attack by the beginning of 1939, building an International Class D machine (2000 cc-3000 cc) using the 3-litre V-12 in a lightened W 154 chassis. This was clad with a very fine aerodynamic body (below) the hull of which recalled the 1938 Grand Prix car, although the wheels were completely enclosed. On a specially prepared stretch of Autobahn between Dessau and Bitterfeld, southwest of Berlin, Caracciola established two new records on 8 and 14 February: a standing-start mile at 127.3 mph and a standing kilometre at 110 mph.

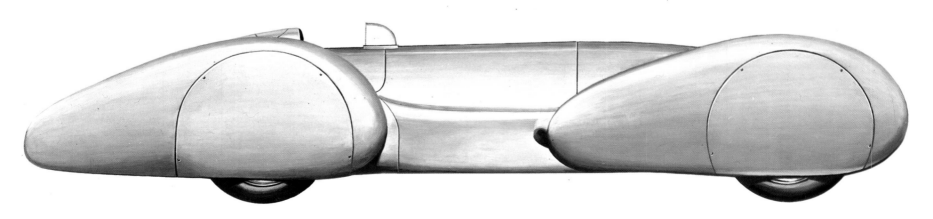

Sick no doubt of seeing German cars always victorious, the Italian sporting authorities announced in September 1938 that all races held in their territories henceforth would be restricted to 1½ litres and that the first of these events would take place at Tripoli on 7 May 1939, Libya having come under Italian control in 1934. Alfa Romeo and Maserati of course hailed this anouncement with delight, both these concerns having great experience of voiturette racing. Daimler-Benz determined to accept the challenge. In November the Racing Department was instructed to build three W 165 chassis and three M 165 engines. For the chassis, the designers drew upon W 154: parallel side members made from oval steel tubes, five tubular cross members, additional bracing being supplied by the rear engine-bearers, as in the W 154; the i.f.s. and De Dion rear end were also similar, while the wheels and brakes were those of the 1939 W 154 scaled down.

Smaller chassis dimensions (wheelbase 8 ft 1 in, front track 5 ft 2 in, rear track 5 ft) and the offset transmission line meant that the driver sat right of centre. If the chassis was W 154 in miniature, this cannot be said of the engine. A short car needs a short power unit, and so a V-8 was chosen, with the banks at 90 degrees, twin o.h.c. per bank and four valves per cylinder. Dimensions were 'over-square' (64 × 58), 1495 cc. Using two carburetters and a single-stage supercharger for each bank this developed 256 bhp at 8000 rpm. Maximum speed exceeded 165 mph. Only two W 165 were built but these, driven by Lang and Caracciola took first and second places in the Tripoli G.P., to the utter dismay of the Italians. The cars appeared but once more, being displayed to the German public during a *tour d'honneur* of the Nürburg Ring before the *Eifelrennen*. Although a few races were held after the outbreak of war, the W 165 never raced again.

The fastest standard car in the world

similar to the old, but with 88 × 111 bore and stroke for a capacity of 5401 cc − hence the name 540. On a c.r. of 5.18:1 it gave 115 bhp unblown, 180 blown. Three from the first batch were supplied to the German government. Designed for state occasions their 'Cabriolet F' bodywork could be used open or closed and had seating for seven. Side panels were reinforced with 4-mm armour-plate and the bullet-proof glass in the windows was one inch (25 mm) thick. There is no record of their being submitted for proof...

The standard models remained in production until the outbreak of war, and performance was even better than that of the 500 series. The two-seater cabriolet 540 K was good for 106 mph and would cruise at 85 mph on an Autobahn, although customers were urged not to use full throttle for very long. In the 540 K Germany prided herself on possessing the fastest standard car in the world, and a motoring writer carolled: 'The marvellous sense of security that one feels at very high speeds is afforded by no other car'. He forgot the heavy steering at parking speeds and the lack of low-speed torque; the richly veneered woodwork, the high-grade leather, and the (standard) set of suitcases took the mind from such things. These cars were not only rapid but safe and forgiving. Unlike the 500/500 K they had direct drive on fourth, but it was still possible to make clutchless changes between the two upper speeds. Gearbox ratios were as follows: first 3.9:1, second 2.28:1, third 1.15:1, in other words a high third, a low second and a gear for restarting on Alps. Two lengths of wheelbase could be had, the same as those of the 500 series.

As late as 1942 the works completed assembly of a few 540 Ks. The very last, according to Factory sources was delivered on 20 July of that year. Pre-war production of the 5.4-litre amounted to 409 cars in all: 97 in 1936, 145 in 1937, 95 in 1938 and 69 in 1939. After 1938 only short-wheelbase models were made.

There was to have been a successor to the 540 K. By 1937 work had begun on an experimental car − W 129

− with aluminium two-seater body and an over-all length of 15 ft 8 in (4480 mm) (as opposed to 18 ft 2 in, 5250 mm, for the 540 K). The prototype clocked 180 kph on test − 112 mph − but war stopped development and three cars which had been completed were made over and sold as standard.

Undoubtedly the best-looking 540 K was the roadster. The two-seater convertible was extremely smart too although not so sleek as the 500K *Autobahn-Kurier* had been. A number of 5.4-litre limousines were built in the Sindelfingen bodyshops of Mercedes-Benz, and it was they who were responsible for a one-off 'shooting-brake', as estate cars were called in 1937.

For the 1939 Motor Show in Berlin Daimler-Benz laid down a small batch of the short-chassis 5.4-litres but with larger bore and shorter stroke (now 95 × 100) giving 5800 cc, known in the drawing-office as W 129 II, and claiming an output, supercharged, of 200 bhp at 3600 rpm. They were unofficially known as 580 K.

The existence of this model has sometimes been doubted, but it was really and truly produced, to the number of twelve examples. The first ten were ready in 1939, the last two experimental cars being completed in 1940. None was ever sold; they were all retained for development work. The chassis numbers earmarked for production cars (449511 − 449540) − engine numbers being identical − were cancelled by managerial decision on 26 August. One 580 engine, its identify confirmed by its number, did however surface ten years later. It was installed in a 540 K. This car is now in the United States. How it reached there is unknown; perhaps it was 'liberated' after the war.

Some mystery also surrounds the 6-litre W 157 called also 600 K, although we know that twenty-three were made in the period 1938 − 1942. Five were bodied as sports cars, the rest as open tourers, Cabriolets B and D, long-chassis limousines or saloons. All these, whether long-chassis or short (11 ft 5 in or 11 ft − 3415 or 3340 mm) bore the suffix K, which seems to have been habitual with the D-B management by this time.

Here as in the case of the 770 there is little doubt that it stood for *Kompressor,* although we have no proof.

The 600 K was slightly shorter than the 770 and there were other recognition features, especially the louvred bonnet. Less well known is the fact that the engine was a V-twelve, of 6020 cc and 'over-square' dimensions, bore and stroke 95 × 82. On a 6:1 c.r. this unit developed some 240 bhp at 3600 rpm. The two-door sporting model weighed almost 2 tons (1980 kg) and would do about 105 mph; it could have been relieved of 200 kg and would then have performed even better. Its five-speed gearbox was of Daimler-Benz manufacture. Work on this model continued through 1941 into 1942 until halted by the war. One wonders whether one of these remarkable Twelves will re-surface. It seemed as though at last some of the lessons of the M-B racing programme 1934-39 had begun to rub off on the production line. There had been little contact between the Racing Department and the main factory up to the war. Pomeroy, Technical Editor of *The Motor,* was walking round the assembly lines on one occasion with Ing. Rudolf Uhlenhaut, chief research engineer on the Racing side, when they came upon a batch of 540Ks being built. 'Good God!' cried Uhlenhaut, 'are they still making *those?*' He was horrified that the lumbering old long-stroke pushrod engines and high megalithic chassis could still be associated with the company that made the most advanced racing cars in the world...

During the war years a few specimens of the 770 and 770K were still built. Since 1937 the *Grosser Mercedes* had possessed a lower chassis fabricated from oval tubes, with independent front suspension and a De Dion rear end as proved on other models, including the 1937 G.P. cars. (The factory's efforts to race with a swing-axle rear end during 1936 for policy reasons had been an almost total failure.) A five-speed gearbox was fitted, with syncromesh on all speeds. The compression ratio of the straight-eight engine was raised to 6:1 so that output rose from 200 bhp at 2800 rpm to 230 bhp at 3200, or 145 without supercharging. Maximum speed was 105 mph. An armoured version of this was produced, measuring 20 ft over all, propelled by a straight eight running at 7:1 compression ratio to give 240 bhp at 3600 and a top speed of about 110 mph. Three-quarter inch (18 mm) armour plate was used, with glass 40 mm thick, and an electromagnetic locking system for the doors.

After the war Daimler-Benz concentrated on the production of the humble side-valve 170V four-cylinder. Luxurious great supercharged cars belonged to a bygone age. Most of those which escaped destruction passed into the hands of U.S. collectors. A few found their way back to Germany, but they seldom come up for sale.

The history of supercharged Mercedes engines would be incomplete without some account of their rôle in Grand Prix racing 1934 – 39. During the early twenties they had been redoubtable enough; in the years before 1939 they achieved virtual supremacy.

The fatal accident to Otto Merz in the SSKL at the Avus in 1933 must have seemed a bad augury for the Stuttgart concern's return to motor racing. But the decision had been made: German cars would be entered once more in what we now call Formula One. Daimler-Benz and the Auto Union combine (Horch, Audi, Wanderer, D.K.W.) each received a subsidy from the new German government amounting to 450,000 Reichmarks. This sum would cover scarcely one-tenth of the cost of designing and building a new racing car, but was encouraging and both teams set to work.

The A.I.A.C.R. (Alliance Internationale des Automobile-Clubs Reconnus) which governed the sport in those days laid down a new Formula for the four seasons 1934 to 1936 inclusive, extended to 1937. Cars must weigh not more than 750 kg – not including driver, fuel, coolant, oil, wheels and tyres, and cockpits must be at least 85 cm (33$^1/_2$ in) in width. At Daimler-Benz a new single-seater was to be designed by Hans Nibel and Max Wagner; Albert Heess and Otto Schill-

The Mercedes-Benz record car with which Caracciola had done 268 mph on a section of Autobahn near Frankfurt emerged for a last appearance at Dessau in 1939. It was no longer powered by a DAB 5.6-litre V-12, but by an M 154 V-12 3-litre, because Daimler-Benz had their eye on International Class D (2000-3000 cc) records. Apart from this engine-change the car (below) was the same as before, a W 154 with very advanced streamlined body in which the only openings were two air inlets at the front and corresponding exits in the sides. On 9 February Rudolf Caracciola launched himself upon Germany's new Bonneville – five miles of Autobahn 100 metres wide built specially for an attempt on the Land Speed Record. Over the flying kilometre he averaged 248.75 mph and for the flying mile almost exactly 250 mph in his 3-litre.

Of all the supercharged Mercedes the car with the longest gestation period and strangest fate must surely be the gigantic T 80 (below). In 1936 Hans Stuck determined to become fastest man in the world. To realise this ambition he would have to beat Sir Malcolm Campbell's record of 301 mph in Bluebird. He approached Ferdinand Porsche, a great friend of his, who at once agreed to have a go. But the only engines powerful enough were those being built in utmost secrecy by Daimler-Benz for the German Air Force. Thanks to contacts in the Supply Department at the Air Ministry Stuck was

promised the loan of two DB 601 aero-engines, and Daimler-Benz agreed to finance the project. During the design stage however two new Land Speed record were set up, first in 1931 by Captain G.E.T. Eyston's Rolls-Royce R-engined Thunderbolt at 312 mph, and then in 1938, when Mercedes-Benz were preoccupied with building Grand Prix cars, by John Cobb's Railton Mobil Special at more than 350 mph. The two engines originally chosen would no longer do. They were replaced by a new experimental unit, the DB 603 V3, which was installed in the multi-tubular T 80 chassis at the beginning of 1939. This engine was an inverted V-12 of 44,500 cc (162 × 180) with centrifugal superchar ger; its power some 3000 bhp. The outbreak of war interrupted preparation of the car. In February 1940 the experimental engine went back to the aero-research department, and the chassis was parked in a lock-up at Untertürckheim. So the three-ton, 27-foot monster (wheelbase 19 feet) never did speed over that special stretch at Dessau in pursuit of Cobb's final record of 394 mph... and Stuck was unable to achieve his ambition.

The noisiest car in the world

ing were to be responsible for the engine, assisted by Georg Scheerer, expert in supercharging.

W 25, first of the new Mercedes-Benz racing cars received a straight-eight engine of 3.3 litres (78 × 88), and a Roots blower running at twice engine speed. Power developed by this 'noisiest car in the world', as *The Autocar* called it, was 325 bhp. This car was successful on its very first outing: on 3 June 1934 Manfred von Brauchitsch won the *Eifelrennen* on the Nürburg Ring, driving what the papers called a Silver Arrow. The name arose in this way: When Brauchitsch presented his car for scrutineering painted white, Germany's racing colour, it was found to be overweight, and when all else failed to bring it within the limit paint was stripped off down to the bare aluminium.

This 'three-three' Mercedes proved no match for Dr Porsche's *P-Wagen* Auto Union and at Stuttgart a replacement was laid down, a straight eight of 4 litres, (82 × 94.5, 3990 cc,) which, once it found its form later in 1934 was to do well both in races and record-breaking. Enthusiasts everywhere bated their breath when Rudolf Caracciola, driving a special enclosed *Rennlimousine* covered the flying kilometre on a new piece of straight road at Gyon in Hungary at 198.75 mph. This drive took place in October, after the Grand Prix season closed, and set a new international Class C kilometre record. It was also the highest speed that had ever been reached on the road. The 4-litre car developed 430 bhp at 5800 rpm – about 107 bhp per litre.

The 1934 season finished with four important races out of eight going to Mercedes. In 1935 they won nine out of fourteen big events. The 1936 cars were far less successful, because for marketing reasons it was decreed that any Mercedes model in the public eye must be equipped with swing-axle suspensions, although the engineers clamoured for De Dion. Auto Union therefore swept the board. In 1937 German cars were triumphant: Mercedes-Benz won seven of the *grandes épreuves*, Auto Union won five. That was the year of W 125, without question the fastest and most reliable of the 750 kg Formula. The heart of the matter was a supercharged straight eight (94 × 102) of 5600 cc giving in racing form nearly 600 bhp and for sprints and records 646 bhp. These were thirsty monsters, and as they did less than 2 m.p.g. and races were run over a distance of 500 kilometres (310 miles) stops for refuelling played an important part in racing.

In 1938 the '750 kg' Formula which, like most new G.P. regulations was intended to make cars slower and safer – and had spectacularly failed to do so although producing the loudest and most exciting cars of all time – was replaced by a new Formula which, in practice, meant a choice between 4$\frac{1}{2}$ litres unblown and 3 litres supercharged, with a maximum weight of 850 kg. Clearly the new Formula favoured supercharged engines, which under the Regulations were required to give 1.5 times as much horsepower per litre as the unblown Talbots and Delahayes whereas in fact they gave nearly double.

The new 3-litre Mercedes, the W 154, was a V-twelve (67 × 70, 2962 cc) with its two banks at 60 degrees and four valves per cylinder. At 7800 rpm it put out almost 470 bhp, or 158 per litre. Mixture was sucked from two carburetters and two Roots blowers providing some 18 lbs boost, although this 'cost' 150 bhp to produce, which must be subtracted from the total. The cylinder heads were not detachable. Mercedes-Benz reinforced their usual strong team of Caracciola, von Brauchitsch and Lang with R.J.B. Seaman, the young Englishman who had done so brilliantly in 1$\frac{1}{2}$-litre racing in 1936 at the wheel of his rejuvenated 1927 G.P. Delage. Richard Seaman gained his first victory for Mercedes-Benz by winning the German G.P. itself on the Nürburg Ring, and Caracciola for the third time became European Champion.

For the 1939 season, the W 154 underwent certain modifications, the most important being a Porsche-developed two-stage blower. This arrangement featured a large Roots blower pumping into a smaller, which fed the carburetter, which combination helped to increase output to 485 at 8000 revs. The European title went to Hermann Lang, who won the Grand Prix of Pau, the *Eifelrennen,* the Belgian G.P., and the Grand Prix of Switzerland on the Bremgarten circuit at Berne. Caracciola took the German G.P.

After the war these cars reappeared. In 1951 Fangio, Kling and Lang took three of them to Argentine but found them little suited to the short twisty circuits They were also handicapped by a lack of suitable fuel, Mercedes having previously run them on their own W.W. mixture, and were twice beaten by Gonzalez in a 2-litre Ferrari in *Formule libre* races at Buenos Aires.

Besides the 1939 3-litre, known as W 163, Mercedes-Benz, working in immense haste in order to beat the Italians who, by changing the Grand Prix of Tripoli to a $1^1/_2$-litre event had hoped to have that rich and glamorous race to themselves, built a team of new 1500s – the W 165.

Completed in very few months, the W 165 had a 1495 cc eight-cylinder engine of over-square dimensions (bore and stroke 64×58), and because a small car must have a short engine this one was a V8, and was also fed by a two-stage supercharger. These very advanced cars ran only once before war stopped play but they won their race, Lang and Caracciola beating all the Alfettas and Maseratis. The W 165 was giving 254 bhp at 8000 rpm, 169 bhp/litre.

When after the war the Fédération Internationale Automobile (which replaced the A.I.A.C.R. as governing body) met to decide upon a new G.P. formula, the supremacy of the German 3-litres was very much in people's minds, and so was the performance of the Tripoli cars. As the unblown $4^1/_2$-litres had clearly been outclassed by the supercharged 3-litres against which they had been pitted, it was decided to give them another chance, this time against supercharged 1.5-litre engines, a capacity ratio of 3:1. Mercedes however had other fish to fry at that moment and, rather sadly, the last acts in the drama of supercharging were played without a Mercedes in the cast.

In 1952 Daimler-Benz announced their return to motor racing, in the sports car category. And for the sports car race at the Nürburg Ring on 2 August the Racing Department undertook an experiment; they fitted superchargers to two of the 3-litre 300 SL sports-racing cars. The blower added some 50 extra horses bringing the total to 230 bhp; but these cars (Kling and Lang) had to run in the over-3-litre class. Their lap-speeds in practice proved disappointing, and no faster than those of the unblown cars. In the race Lang and Kling drove standard unsupercharged machines. And those who had expected Mercedes to enter the Carrera Panamericana with supercharged cars were obliged to think again: the days of the supercharged Mercedes were gone. When Mercedes returned briefly to dominate once again the Grand Prix scene in 1954-55, the formula required 2.5 litres, with no such adventitious aids.

However. The dream of every collector of Vintage and Classic cars must be to own a supercharged Mercedes or Mercedes-Benz. Very few live out their dream. It is not just that the prices are high – a 500 K or 540 K now costs many times its value when new – but these cars have become so rare that it may be years before one is available. And it is not merely nostalgia that makes owners reluctant to sell, but something deeper than that. As the SSK catalogue put it in 1931: 'Victorious on all the leading circuits in Europe, winner of many international *concours d'élégance,* and admired at every fashionable rendezvous, this motor car is the very embodiment of perfection in automobile design... its entrancing beauty and breeding make it the noblest representative of the oldest automobile factory in the world'.

Nothing could better present the Supercharged Mercedes image except the gleaming metal of the car itself and the eldritch scream of its blower in full cry. As a famous Mercedes salesman remarked to a customer: 'The sex-appeal of the exhaust-note alone, dear boy, is worth *twice* the asking price'.

What a contrast is here between the 3-litre W 154 of 1938 and the 1939 W 165 1¹/₂-litre voiturette built for Tripoli! Long, low and formidable, Lang's car, photographed in the French Grand Prix at Rheims, gives a great impression of power and speed. The 1500 cc V-8, pictured here on its initial tests at Hockenheim in April 1939, was short, neat and, according to Richard Seaman, almost boringly easy to drive.

Daimler-Benz engineers designed, built and ▷ tested the W 165 in a mere eight months. It was the second 1¹/₂-litre Grand Prix car and the first V-8 in the company's history.

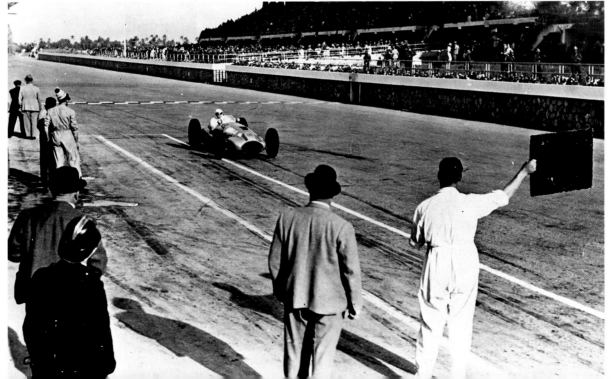

On 7 May 1939 the 1¹/₂-litre W 165 made its first – and only – appearance in international racing, pitted against the Alfa Romeo and Maserati voiturettes at Tripoli. Lang made short work of the opposition, to win at 122.9 mph, closely followed by Caracciola.

MERCEDES AND MERCEDES-BENZ SUPERCHARGED ENGINES 1919-1952

Model		Chassis	Engine	Cyl.	Bore/Stoke	c.c.	bhp	rpm	Valve arrang.	Production
	10/30*	–	–	4	80 × 130	2612	35	2000	sl. v.	1919-1921
	28/95	–	–	6	105 × 140	7250	140	2000	O.h.c.	1920-1924
	10/40/65	–	–	4	80 × 130	2612	65	2000	O.h.c.	1921-1924
	6/25/40	–	–	4	68 × 108	1568	40	2800	2 O.h.c.	1921-1924
	6/40/65	–	–	4	65 × 113	1499	65	2800	2 O.h.c.	1922-1923
Indianapolis		–	M 7294	4	70 × 129	1989	95	4500	2 O.h.c.	1923
	130/150	–	M 218	8	61.7 × 82.8	1980	170	7000	2 O.h.c.	1924
600	24/100/140	W 9456	M 9456	6	94 × 150	6240	140	3000	O.h.c.	1924-1929
400	15/70/100	W 836	M 836	6	80 × 130	3920	100	3100	O.h.c.	1924-1929
200	8/40/60	W 6506/I K	M 6506 K	6	65 × 100	1988	60	3500	s.v.	1924-1927
300 K	12/60/90	W 67058	M 67058	8	67 × 105	2960	90	3550	O.h.c.	1926
600 K	24/100/140	W 9456	M 9456	6	94 × 150	6240	140	3200	O.h.c.	1927-1929
620	24/110/160	W 9456/I	M 9456/I	6	94 × 150	6240	160	3100	O.h.c.	1927-1929
630 K	24/110/160	W 9456/II	M 9456/I	6	94 × 150	6240	160	3100	O.h.c.	1927-1932
660 K	25/130/220	W 98456	M 98456	6	98 × 145	6559	220	3100	O.h.c.	1927-1933
680 K	26/130/180	W 9856	M 9856	6	98 × 150	6789	180	3000	O.h.c.	1927-1928
680 K	26/145/270	W 1456	M 1456	6	100 × 145	6830	270	3100	O.h.c.	1927-1931
630	24/100/140	W 9456/II	M 9456 Sp.	6	94 × 150	6240	145	3000	O.h.c.	1928-1931
680 S	26/120/180	W 9856	M 9856	6	98 × 150	6800	180	3000	O.h.c.	1927-1928
680 S	26/140/180	W 9856 S	M S9856	6	98 × 150	6800	180	3300	O.h.c.	1928
680 S	26/170/225	W 06	M 06	6	98 × 150	6800	225	3300	O.h.c.	1928-1930
680 S	26/190/250	W 06 II	M 06 S	6	98 × 150	6800	250	3300	O.h.c.	1929
700 SS	27/140/200	W 1156 S	M 1156 S	6	100 × 150	7065	200	3300	O.h.c.	1927-1928
710 SS	27/160/200	W 1156 S/II	M 1156 S/II	6	100 × 150	7065	200	3300	O.h.c.	1928-1930
710 SS	27/170/225	W 06	M 06	6	100 × 150	7065	225	3300	O.h.c.	1928-1935
710 SS	27/180/250	W 06 S	M 06 S	6	100 × 150	7065	250	3300	O.h.c.	1929-1930
720 SSK	27/170/225	W 06/III	M 06	6	100 × 150	7065	225	3300	O.h.c.	1928-1934
720 SSK	27/180/250	W S06	M S06	6	100 × 150	7065	250	3300	O.h.c.	1928-1933
720 SSKL	27/240/300	W 06 RS	M 06 RS	6	100 × 150	7065	300	3400	O.h.c.	1929-1934
770 K	30/150/200	W 07 K	M 07 K	8	95 × 135	7655	200	2800	Pushrod	1930-1938
380	15/90/120	W 22	M 22	8	78 × 100	3820	120	3400	Pushrod	1933-1934
380 K	15/90/140	W 22	M 22 K	8	78 × 100	3820	140	3600	Pushrod	1933-1934
500 K		W 24	M 24	8	86 × 108	5019	160	3400	Pushrod	1933-1935
500 K		W 29	M 24/I	8	86 × 108	5019	160	3400	Pushrod	1934-1936
540 K		W 24	M 24/II	8	88 × 111	5401	180	3400	Pushrod	1934-1935
540 K		W 29	M 24/II	8	88 × 111	5401	180	3400	Pushrod	1936-1939
540 K		W 129	M 24/II	8	88 × 111	5401	180	3400	Pushrod	1936-1939
770		W 150	M 150	8	95 × 135	7655	230	3200	Pushrod	1938-1942
770 K		W 150/II	M 150/II	8	95 × 135	7655	240	3600	Pushrod	1938-1942
600 K		W 157	M 157	12	82 × 95	6020	240	3600	O.h.c.	1938-1942
580 K		W 129/II	M 124	8	95 × 100	5800	200	3400	Pushrod	1939-1940

RACING CARS AND RECORD-BREAKERS

Model		Chassis	Engine	Cyl.	Bore/Stoke	c.c.	bhp	rpm	Valve arrang.	Production
750 kg Grand Prix		W 25	M 25A	8	78 × 88	3360	354	5500	2 O.h.c.	1934
750 kg Grand Prix		W 25	M 25AB	8	82 × 88	3710	398	5800	2 O.h.c.	1934
750 kg Grand Prix		W 25	M 25B	8	82 × 94.5	3990	430	5800	2 O.h.c.	1934-1935
750 kg Grand Prix		W 25	M 25C	8	82 × 102	4310	462	5500	2 O.h.c.	1935
750 kg Grand Prix		W 25	ME 25	8	86 × 102	4740	453	5800	2 O.h.c.	1935-1936
750 kg Grand Prix		W 25	DAB	12	82 × 88	5577	616	5800	4 O.h.c.	1936-1938
Record		W 125	DAB	12	82 × 88	5577	616	5800	4 O.h.c.	1937-1938
750 kg Grand Prix		W 125	ME 25	8	86 × 102	4740	453	5800	2 O.h.c.	1937
750 kg Grand Prix		W 125	M 125 (F)	8	94 × 102	5660	488	5500	2 O.h.c.	1937
3 litres Grand Prix		W 154	M 154 (H)	12	67 × 70	2962	427	8000	4 O.h.c.	1937-1939
3 litres Grand Prix		W 154	M 163 (K)	12	67 × 70	2962	480	8000	4 O.h.c.	1939
3 litres Grand Prix		W 154	M154/R108	12	67 × 70	2962	495	7800	4 O.h.c.	1939
1.5 litre Tripoli cars		W 165	M 165	8	64 × 58	1495	256	8000	4 O.h.c.	1939
300 SL Sports racing		W 194	M 197	6	85 × 88	2996	230	6400	2 O.h.c.	1952

O.h.c. = Overhead camshaft   s.v. = side valves   Pushrod = Pushrod overhead valves   sl.v. = sleeve valves

* Experimental only, production cars unsupercharged

PHOTOGRAPHIC ACKNOWLEDGEMENTS

Page 6: Daimler-Benz ● 13: Süddeutscher Verlag (above, left), Max Bickel (above, right), National Motor Museum Beaulieu (below) ● 17: Edita ● 23: Daimler-Benz ● 26: Harrah's Automobile Collection (above, left), Daimler-Benz ● 27: National Motor Museum, Beaulieu ● 29: Daimler-Benz (above, left), Süddeutscher Verlag (above, left), Daimler-Benz (below) ● 32: Süddeutscher Verlag ● 33: Edita (above), Daimler-Benz (below) ● 36: Archiv Vaclav Petrick ● 37: Süddeutscher Verlag (above, left), Süddeutscher Verlag (above, right), Edita (below) ● 40: Edita (above), Automobil Revue (below) ● 44: Daimler-Benz ● 45: Süddeutscher Verlag ● 47: Daimler-Benz ● 54: Süddeutscher Verlag (above, left), Süddeutscher Verlag (above, right), Automobilhistorischer Bilderdienst (below) ● 55: Automobilhistorischer Bilderdienst ● 57: Automobil revue ● 60: Automobil Revue (above), Süddeutscher Verlag (below) ● 61: Daimler-Benz ● 64: Süddeutscher Verlag (above left), Daimler-Benz ● 66: Süddeutscher Verlag (above), National Motor Museum, Beaulieu (centre), Daimler-Benz (below) ● 67: Daimler-Benz ● 70: Daimler-Benz (above, left + right), Süddeutscher Verlag (centre), Daimler-Benz (below) ● 73: Daimler-Benz, Ullstein Bilderdienst (below) ● 77: Daimler-Benz, Süddeutscher Verlag (below) ● 81: Daimler-Benz ● 92: Günther Molter (above, centre), Daimler-Benz (below) ● 93: Daimler-Benz.

ACKNOWLEDGEMENTS

The authors and the publisher would like to thank all those who help them gather documents and pictures for this book, and in particular Günther Molter and Bernard Hülsen of Daimler-Benz AG; Nick Georgano of the National Motor Museum, Beaulieu; Hans-Heinrich von Fersen; Michael Sedgwick and Karl Ludvigsen.

This book was published under the
direction of
Ami Guichard

Editorial responsibility and supervision by Tim Chilvers

Produced under the direction of Charles Riesen

Designed by Mario Fasoletti

Printed by G.E.A. Milan
and bound by Maurice Busenhart Lausanne
Printed in Italy